Uncle Jack's
OUTERBANKS

BY JACK SANDBERG

Uncle Jack's Outer Banks: The Ultimate Collection

OUT OF PRINT
Uncle Jack's Outer Banks: A Pretty Funny Book (1982)
Uncle Jack's Outer Banks: Part II ... The Sequel (1992)
Uncle Jack's Outer Banks (1998)

Uncle Jack's OUTER BANKS

THE ULTIMATE COLLECTION

JACK SANDBERG

BEACH GLASS
BOOKS

Published by Beach Glass Books
Manufactured in the United States of America
First Printing 2020

Front and back cover drawings by Mike Lucas
Front cover colorization by Vicki McAllister
Author photograph supplied by the author
Book and cover design by Ray McAllister

Jack Sandberg, 1930-
Uncle Jack's Outer Banks: The Ultimate Collection /
        by Jack Sandberg
ISBN 978-0-9987881-7-3

To my beloved wife,
Susan Patricia Sandberg

CONTENTS

PREFACE

THE WIT AND WISDOM of "Uncle Jack" first appeared in print on April 15, 1980, in the premier issue of the *Outer Banks Current*, a weekly newspaper published in Manteo, North Carolina. The author was a former college professor who had been lured away from a sinecure at Carnegie Mellon University in Pittsburgh by the irresistible charms of life in the then laid-back town of Nags Head whose acquaintance he had made ten years earlier.

After that first stay in the picturesque old First Colony Inn on the oceanfront in 1970 he began an obsessive search for a way to trade the smoky environs of Pittsburgh for the fresh air and sunshine of the Outer Banks. Opportunity finally knocked in the summer of 1979 when a friend told him that a group of local investors were planning to start a weekly newspaper to rival the venerable *Coastland Times* which they felt was entirely too much tilted toward support of the local Democratic political regime.

While it would result in a 50 percent pay cut and a tortuous realignment of his political underpinnings he applied for and got the job of reporter for the fledgling *Current* to start in the

Spring of 1980. For the first issue he contributed what would become a regular feature of the paper throughout most of its ten-year life—the musings of "Uncle Jack"—a somewhat crotchety old guy who tempered his often acerbic comments with a sly sense of humor. (His inspiration for the third-person format was the clever syndicated columnist Judith Martin whose "Miss Manners" lit up the pages of hundreds of newspapers across the U.S.)

Early days at the *Current* were chaotic with the owners hiring and firing no fewer than three editors in the first few months. Finally Uncle Jack himself volunteered to act as editor on a temporary basis while they searched for an experienced and competent journalist to take over the reins. This was accomplished after a few months during

Sue and Jack Sandberg in the Yellowhouse Gallery in the 1990s.

which Uncle Jack managed to alienate several key
advertisers and bring the paper to the brink of
insolvency.

With the *Current* finally in good hands Uncle
Jack resigned from his reportorial position but
offered to provide management with a column
each week as a trade-out for an advertisement
for his then-spouse's business, Yellowhouse
Gallery in Nags Head. This turned out to be a
mutually beneficial arrangement for most of the
next decade, almost up until the paper ceased
publication in March of 1990.

When a new weekly paper called the *Outer
Banks Sentinel* began publication in 1996 the
staff, some of whom had worked at the *Current*,
plied him with drink and otherwise enticed him,
primarily with flattery, to resume writing his
column under a similar agreement which he did for
several years.

In 2005 he commenced writing a blog for
a website called the *OBX Connection* which he
continued to do for more than ten years. The
archive of those blog entries has been accessed by
readers well over a million times.

During his stints with the *Sentinel* and
Current Uncle Jack self-published three paperback
collections of his columns which he sold primarily
in the gallery (or gave as gifts to big spenders).
These publications have long been out of print
although used copies still turn up on Amazon and

elsewhere, usually at greatly inflated prices. Uncle Jack is grateful to publisher Ray McAllister for adding this new collection of his columns to the prestigious roster of Beach Glass Books. Enjoy.

JACK SANDBERG
Baltimore, Maryland

INTRODUCTION

THE OUTER BANKS of North Carolina are everyone's idea of fun. No less an authority than TripAdvisor (in today's world, you know, TripAdvisor probably *is* a top authority) has declared the Outer Banks the Number 1 "Family-Friendly Beach" in all of the United States. So, fun, yes.

But not many think of the OBX as funny.

Save one.

I became aware of Jack Sandberg in the early 1980s, seeing a small book of his columns from the *Outer Banks Current* weekly newspaper. They were indeed funny—very funny and very savvy. Jack, it would turn out, was hugely popular on the Outer Banks. He wrote critically and wryly but always affectionately about this beloved and oh-so-vulnerable strip of islands.

Jack's book, which I found in a small shop in Kill Devil Hills, was a yellow booklet of but 32 pages and costing but $2.75, with an intriguingly odd cover sketch of a sleeping man fishing from the deck of a house, a bottle of Rebel Yell beside his rocker. The title—*Uncle Jack's Outer Banks*—came with a subversively modest subtitle, *A Pretty Funny Book*.

On the back, "Uncle Jack" had written "Dear Person" this: "A lot of people have told Uncle Jack that reading his column is the high point of the week for them which is just about the saddest thing he ever heard. That should give you some idea of how dull it can get around here, especially in winter."

But "strange people" kept telling him he should put them in a book, he continued. "After a while that started to sound like a good idea to Uncle Jack because as long as he can remember he has been trying to figure out some way to get rich and famous without working. Maybe this book will do the trick. Uncle Jack is terrible at arithmetic but he figured out that if only one million people would buy ..."

He had me. I plunked down the $2.75 plus tax.

But what was this third-person deal?

I would not find out until years later, in 2000, while interviewing Sandberg for the *Richmond Times-Dispatch*, the first of at least five occasions in which I milked Jack's natural humor for my own column. "I'll tell you who was the greatest influence," he said over the phone. "Miss Manners, who was writing in that style. But she was already using the name 'Miss Manners,' so I had to choose something else."

Fair enough. Jack's advice was dead-on but hardly about etiquette. It was more likely advice to vacationers on when to go to the ABC store to avoid traffic on the Bypass, say—or to oceanfront home buyers who didn't realize they should never make longterm plans. That sort of "advice." Sometimes churlish, to be sure. But always delivered with a wink.

Along the way, Jack also became an important voice in the Outer Banks. This can't be overstated. Not every developer or real estate agent or even government official may have appreciated his voice, but Jack found humorous ways to jumpstart discussions on overcrowding, unthinking development,* and what was then called "erosion." (Erosion, he noted, was merely the natural moving around of sand. It only mattered if you built on the sand. If you actually built on the sand right by the ocean, he said, Mother Nature was coming after you. Your choice.)

Jack had first seen the Outer Banks as a young Navy man stationed at Norfolk, Virginia. He often "bragged" in print about being a high school graduate, but in fact he had graduated from the University of Wisconsin, gone on to graduate school at the University of Virginia, then taught for 17 years at Carnegie Mellon University.

But his heart was in the Outer Banks. "I started coming here while I was living in Pittsburgh," he told me in 2000. "The first time I was here, I was here no more than a day when I discovered this is where I would like to live. That was 1970. It took me ten years to figure out how to do that."

* There had been a few attempts to mitigate ravages of nature and over-development. Two early examples: the Cape Hatteras National Seashore opened in the 1950s, keeping much of Hatteras and Ocracoke islands in a near-natural state. And the Town of Nags Head began zoning and land use planning, with mixed results, in the early 1960s.

The answer: he ran into people starting a newspaper. That simple. Soon, beginning in 1980, Jack's alter ego became a local legend in the pages of the little *Outer Banks Current.*

"Uncle Jack" wrote weekly columns for the better part of a decade, took a few years off, and returned to write well into the 21st century for a new weekly newspaper, *The Outer Banks Sentinel,* as the *Current* had disappeared. *The Sentinel,* which would itself disappear in 2019, knew where its bread was buttered. If you wanted to read Uncle Jack back in the early 2000s, forget going online. You had to buy the newspaper. The rest of the paper was free. Not Uncle Jack's columns.

Smartly, Jack kept the rights to his colums, however, and published two more *Uncle Jack's Outer Banks* booklets in the 1990s. (He brilliantly subtitled the second, *Part II ... The Sequel.* By the time of the third, he may have run out of brilliance. The book has no subtitle.) For his day job, he co-ran Yellowhouse Gallery, selling artworks and later adding a framing shop.

Years later, I would meet Jack. I had written books on Hatteras Island and Ocracoke and intended something similar on the Nags Head area. Tooling around in his yellow Mini Cooper convertible, he showed me all the gone-but-not-forgotten spots and where lines of houses had fallen into the sea. It was a guided tour I'll never forget.

Jack was no longer writing a newspaper column

then—though he did still craft online pieces about his travels elsewhere—and I later grabbed him to write about the Outer Banks a couple times when I was editing *Boomer* magazine in Richmond.

But otherwise his works were mostly unavailable.

A funny voice lost.

A truthful voice lost.

Two decades into the 21st century, I got in touch with him to suggest republishing. If he wouldn't, I could. (By now, I had added publishing to writing.) In May 2019, my wife Vicki and I met his wife Sue and him at their South Nags Head home.

He offered us Rolling Rock, his go-to beer.

I offered him a standard author contract.

He countered with a shocker: how about if he sold me the rights to all his works?

At his age, and with his health concerns, Jack joked, he couldn't wait around to collect royalties. In fact, Sue and he were in the process of selling their home to be nearer her daughter and to Johns Hopkins Hospital.

So for a generously low upfront price (thanks, Jack), he sold the rights to his works and accompanying cartoons. He gave me files of yellowing newspaper clippings. He agreed to send photos of himself and to write a new preface.

This resulting collection is not truly representative of his entire work. Jack wrote more than 1,000 columns and, perhaps surprisingly, most were *not* much about the Outer Banks. Columnists on deadline often grab the best available topic, you see. His books, too, had included many non-OBX pieces.

I had the luxury to pick and choose from all his works, and thus this collection *is* focused on the Outer Banks. It is larger than his three booklets combined and includes many pieces not seen in three or four decades.

Nothing here is chronological, by the way. Many columns literally are timeless, and indeed Jack often re-used his columns several times. ("Uncle Jack strongly believes in recycling and he has no shame," he once admitted.) It doesn't matter when he wrote them. Often, to be frank, it was impossible to tell, anyway.

I've done little editing, other than making some trims and minor changes required by the passage of time. Something else I found: Jack seemed to hate ... commas. Really. Commas. Perhaps he thought they cost extra. I started inserting them. Then I gave up. Without them, his sentences have a nice run-on style. A conversational style that I'm sure he intended. It *feels* as if he is talking to you.

Which he is.

Uncle Jack also is a master at what can best be called understated hyperbole. *Understated hyperbole.* It would seem an oxymoron, this pairing of two antonyms. Yet Uncle Jack often calmly describes what he considers an explosive situation. Tell me who else, for example, would describe himself this way:

Uncle Jack is the kind of person who tries to look on the bright side of every ecological disaster ...

Or what experienced shopkeeper would describe his business philosophy quite like this:

He has watched the same toddlers who once threatened to lay waste to his entire inventory grow up to be doctors and lawyers and computer programmers and other forms of solvent adults—all with a highly developed appreciation for expensive antique prints and maps. He has to confess that there were times when he wanted to kill them but it does prove that in business it is a good idea to think of what is best in the long term.

Finally, Jack is, to pull out another oxymoron, a clear-eyed sentimentalist. His love of the Outer Banks is full-hearted, and full-throated, but nonetheless he worries ...

Well, you'll find out.

If you've read Uncle Jack before, you know what sheer *fun* you're in for (as are people near you, because you're bound to read aloud to them). And if you haven't, you're in for a treat, especially if you love the Outer Banks. And laughter.

So welcome, everyone, to Uncle Jack's world.

The Outer Banks have never been so inviting.

RAY McALLISTER
Richmond, Virginia

Thank God It's Wednesday

Back when Uncle Jack was the editor of a small weekly newspaper, Wednesday afternoon was always the high water mark in the toilet bowl of his week. That was because the paper "went to press," as they say in the journalism racket, at noon on Wednesday.

By noon on Wednesday, there was nothing more that Uncle Jack could do to, or for, the *Outer Banks Current*. The world could come to an end at 12:01 p.m. on Wednesday but the *Current's* readers wouldn't find out about it until a week from Thursday.

Maybe that is why Uncle Jack always felt like going fishing on Wednesday afternoons. He could waste time on his favorite fishing pier without feeling like he should be doing something more worthwhile like writing another editorial about the Oregon Inlet crisis or cleaning the rust out from under his typewriter.

When he remembers what those Wednesday afternoons on the fishing pier were usually like, though, he wonders why he kept doing it. Fishing is something he is not terrifically good at, like he is at sitting on the porch and rocking, for example.

Uncle Jack is so bad at fishing that they even started kidding him about it over at the fishing pier. Every time they saw Uncle Jack coming with his plastic bucket full of rusty tackle and his Kmart rod and reel they would say, "Here comes Uncle Jack— must be time for the fish to stop biting" and other humorous things like that.

Uncle Jack would make believe he didn't hear any of that stuff and he would go right on out to his favorite place at the end of the pier where he came very close to catching a fish once back in 1978. The rest of it would usually go something like this:

Uncle Jack squeezes in between an eight-year-old boy and his grandmother who are bottom fishing and he reaches into his plastic bucket for his trusty reel and white jerk jigger with the hooks that are hardly rusty at all. He is not quite sure how he snags the back of his hand on the same Hopkins every time he reaches in the bucket but that is what he does.

Little boy and grandmother watch carefully while Uncle Jack unhooks the only thing he will catch all afternoon—his own hand.

Pretty soon the bleeding stops and Uncle Jack is ready to cast. With an easy flick of the wrist he propels his beloved red and white jigger toward the horizon.

"Pop" goes Uncle Jack's line. "Splash" goes Uncle Jack's jerk jigger as it joins the millions of dollars worth of tackle—much of it his own—already lining the bottom around his favorite fishing pier. Uncle Jack makes a mental note that the cost of his next fish, if he ever catches one, has just gone up by $2.39.

Noticing that the little boy and grandmother each caught two nice fish while he was trying to get the Hopkins out of his hand, Uncle Jack decides to try bottom fishing for a while. He starts hacking up the mullet that has already added another $1.50 to the cost of the fish he might catch sometime and tries to force a couple of pieces onto the rusty hooks of his bottom rig. Uncle Jack will never understand why hooks that won't go through mullet skin seem to go right into his own thumb so easy.

With a beautiful, lazy underhand toss Uncle Jack puts his bottom rig right where he wants it—twenty yards straight out from the pier. Unfortunately this is directly over grandmother's line which he finds out when grandmother hooks another croaker and everything gets tangled into such a mess it takes Uncle Jack twenty minutes to get it all straightened out again. Uncle Jack tries to remember his own sainted mother while he listens to this old crone yell at him that people who don't know how to fish shouldn't be allowed on fishing piers and other things that he couldn't print in a family newspaper.

For the next two hours, chunk by luscious chunk of mullet, Uncle Jack enriches the lives of countless truly needy crabs who thank him by tangling themselves in his hooks at every opportunity.

Finally, tired and weak with thirst, Uncle Jack tosses his bottom rig, loaded with his last two pieces of sun-dried mullet, as far as he can in what he is sure is a final, futile effort.

He barely has time to take in the slack when "WHAM" he gets a strike so hard it almost pulls the pole out of his hands. Uncle Jack fumbles with the tension control on his corroded Gaylord Perry signature reel but as usual he is too slow. "Pop" goes his line for the second time.

"What happened, Mister?" asks the little boy.

When Is an Island Not an Island?

Dear Uncle Jack,

I enjoyed my visit to the Outer Banks last month but I got very confused because I kept seeing signs that said "Bodie Island," "Pea Island" and "Hatteras Island" but I never could find any islands. Does "island" mean something different on the Outer Banks than it does in different places?

Geography Major,
Chapel Hill

"I don't know, son," says Uncle Jack in his best John Wayne voice, "but I think I just lost the biggest king mackerel I ever saw."

Uncle Jack didn't get away with it though because some good ole boy in a Junior Johnson Pit Crew T-shirt heard what he said and he took his Budweiser can out of his mouth long enough to say, "King mackerel, my a—. That was a f——g skate broke his line."

After that final insult Uncle Jack picks up his plastic bucket, lighter now by $6 worth of bait and tackle, and heads for home. He feels calm, relaxed, refreshed and ready to face another strenuous week as editor of a small weekly newspaper.

Nothing restores the soul quite like fishing. Uncle Jack knows.

(OBX)

Dear Major,

You have unwittingly discovered one more example of the wisdom, frugality and patience of the hardy folk who settled this fragile strand known as the Outer Banks. Bodie Island (pronounced "body" as in Raquel Welch) and all the other non-islands you name really were islands at one time. When the inlets filled up and they weren't islands any more nobody bothered to change the signs because everybody who lives here knows that one of these days—maybe next week— they're going to be islands again.

Geodetically,
Uncle Jack

Thanks a Lot

One thing Uncle Jack is always thankful for on Thanksgiving is that he is not in the fourth grade with Mrs. Stonebreaker any more.

Mrs. Stonebreaker always managed to wreck every holiday by making everybody write an essay about it and Thanksgiving was no exception.

On Thanksgiving she made you write about what you were thankful for and that was not easy because when Uncle Jack was in Mrs. Stonebreaker's class the only thing he was thankful for was weekends.

He was too smart to put that in his essay, though, and that is the main reason he is a high school graduate today.

Also it was hard to write a good essay in Mrs. Stonebreaker's class because she was always coming up behind you and rapping your knuckles with a ruler if you held your pencil wrong or committed some other terrible crime against humanity like that.

Anyway, Uncle Jack is going to stop thinking about that because it was a long time ago and the scars on his knuckles have healed up pretty good and he has many things to be thankful for now besides Saturdays and Sundays.

To start with he still has all the things he was thankful for last Thanksgiving, but this year he has something new to be thankful for which is his new secondhand Jeep.

Uncle Jack is not kidding when he tells you his new secondhand Jeep is the most important thing that has happened in his life since HBO.

For one thing it has turned him from a terrible fisherman into a good fisherman practically overnight.

Back before he got his new secondhand Jeep, Uncle Jack would have to park his old red van on the other side of the dune and then he would have to lug his beer cooler and his chair and his sandwiches and the other stuff you need for fishing over to the water and by the time he got through with all that hauling he was almost too tired to twist a cap much less catch a fish.

Now he just puts everything he needs for fishing right in the back of his new secondhand Jeep and drives the whole works right up to the edge of the water and he still has plenty of energy left to fish when he gets there.

The best part is that he can just keep on driving down the beach until he comes to a person who is catching fish and then he stops his Jeep right there and starts fishing right next to him or her as the case may be.

Uncle Jack is not saying he knows everything there is to know about fishing but he does know the First Rule: Keep driving until you come to where the fish are.

Even when the fish are not biting anywhere it is nice to have a new secondhand Jeep because you can always drive around on the beach and look for interesting trash.

A couple of weeks ago Uncle Jack found a very nice empty yogurt carton with Chinese writing on it which he is going to hang on his Christmas tree and afterwards he will donate it to the Dare County Library so other less fortunate people can enjoy it, too.

Even if you do not run across any interesting trash you can still learn a lot by driving on the beach, Uncle Jack knows.

One thing you can learn about is erosion and that is a very good thing to know about because you never can tell when some realtor is going to sneak up on you and try to sell you some oceanfront property.

When you drive in some places around here you have to be careful not to run into the old foundations and fireplaces of cottages that used to be behind the dune when they were built but now they are right out on the beach.

When you see something like that you do not have to be a high school graduate like Uncle Jack to figure out which way our local ocean is moving.

Which reminds him of one more thing he has to be thankful for—namely that he did not have enough money to buy the oceanfront lot in South Nags Head he was drooling over back in 1970. That very same lot is somewhere out in the ocean today and Uncle Jack is very glad he did not own it when it disappeared.

When it comes to oceanfront property, *caveat emptor* beats *carpe diem* every time if you ask Uncle Jack.

(OBX)

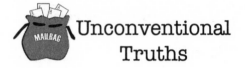

Unconventional Truths

Dear Uncle Jack,

I read in the paper the other day where a lot of experts in the tourist trade agreed that Dare County was never going to amount to anything tourist-wise until they got a real convention center down here. I never heard of a convention center and I was hoping you could tell me what it is.

Common Mann
Mann's Harbor

Dear Common,

Uncle Jack will be happy to answer your question. This is something he knows a lot about because he used to go to a lot of conventions before he moved to the Outer Banks and stopped going anywhere.

He can tell you that a convention is where a group of people who are all in the same line of work will get together some place once a year to talk about what is new in their profession. For instance if you were in the plumbing business you would go to the plumbers' convention to find out what kind of new valves and washers the Japanese have come out with since last year. Or if you are in the car business you go to a convention to find out what new engines Toyota or Honda have come out with and so on.

That is not the only reason people go to conventions though. Uncle Jack found out a long time ago that the main reason why many people go to conventions is that they can go to someplace where nobody knows them and they can fool around a little and also take it off their income tax.

People spend a lot of money when they go to conventions which is why so many towns have convention centers now. If you want conventions to come to your town you have to have a convention center with a room big enough so everybody can all sit down at one time together and eat rubber chicken and listen to boring speeches. This is how they keep from feeling too guilty about leaving their wives and children and going to the convention in the first place.

Anyway if Dare County does get a convention center then maybe instead of going to some warm, sunny place like Las Vegas in January and February the way they do now, some conventions might want to come to Dare County instead. Right off hand Uncle Jack cannot personally think of anybody in his right mind who would rather come to Dare County in the winter but there are large numbers of crazy people in the U.S. so you never know. When he lived in Pittsburgh he used to read about some people called the Polar Bear Club who went swimming in the Monongahela River every New Year's Day when the temperature was usually about four degrees above zero.

Maybe they would like to have their convention here in January or February.

Uncle Jack is not sure if the masochists are organized yet but if they ever have a convention they would surely want to have it here in the winter. They could do all kinds of fun things like hiking to the top of Jockey's Ridge in the nude during a northeaster and letting the sand tear the skin off their bodies.

If you want to know the truth, though, Uncle Jack is not too crazy about the idea of having a lot of conventions around here in the winter. He kind of likes having a few weeks out of the year when he does not have to wait 20 minutes to make a left turn onto the Bypass. Also he is worried about what will happen when the gulls start dropping their clams on the convention center parking lot when it is full of cars. Who is going to pay for all those broken windshields?

This is why Uncle Jack does not think a convention center is anything Dare County needs to rush into right now—unless they want to give him the windshield replacement concession over there.

Opportunistically,
Uncle Jack

The Adventures of Uncle Jack

The Governor Gets To Meet Uncle Jack

Uncle Jack is glad to tell you that he had a very nice time in Chapel Hill last week when he went over there to get his Second Place Award*. He thinks he better tell you about the high points of his trip before he forgets what they were.

First of all he will tell you that Governor Hunt showed up to hand out the award just like they said he would. Uncle Jack got to look at the back of the governor's head for quite a while and also he got

---

* NOTE: Uncle Jack was honored by the North Carolina Press Association for his column writing—this is true—though he scarcely mentions the award here in writing, ostensibly, about being given the award. Fortunately he did explain this in an earlier column: "It was just a second prize but Uncle Jack thought that was pretty good for an amateur. If you are wondering how a person like Uncle Jack who gets paid for writing his column can still think of himself as an amateur, then you have never seen Uncle Jack's paycheck."

to shake his hand one time.

He is happy to report that Governor Hunt has a very neat haircut and a nice firm handshake so if you ask Uncle Jack he ought to make us a perfectly good senator.

The next high point of his trip was the big Awards Party where they had many large tables loaded with good food such as bourbon and gin and olives and chicken wings and you could have as much as you wanted and it was all free.

Uncle Jack probably does not have to tell you how much he enjoyed that part of his trip to Chapel Hill—and especially the chicken wings.

But you might be surprised when he tells you that the free party was not the best part. The best part was that he got to stay at the Europa Hotel and he can tell you that if you think the Armada Inn in Nags Head is something then you have never stayed in the Europa Hotel in Chapel Hill and that's for sure.

For one thing the lobby in the Europa Hotel is bigger than Roller World and Roller Galaxy put together and it is filled with comfortable sofas and overstuffed chairs where you can sit and watch rich people go by all day long if you want to.

Uncle Jack was afraid they would throw him out when he walked into the Europa Hotel wearing his moldy brown suit and his frazzled tie but everybody was nice to him the whole time he was there.

He figures they must have learned it pays to be nice, even to seedy looking persons like Uncle

Jack, because for all they know he could be Howard Hughes or Mick Jagger or somebody like that and if they were not nice to him he might buy the whole place and fire them all on the spot.

Anyway, after the big party Uncle Jack and his award-winning friends decided to stay in the hotel for dinner so no policeman could have the fun of arresting them for driving while impaired. Lucky for them there is no law against crawling while impaired so they got to the Europa Hotel restaurant OK and they were glad they did, too.

It turns out to be one of those very nice restaurants where they give you four different forks and three different spoons and the menu is in some foreign language so you are never quite sure what you are having until they put the plate down in front of you and sometimes even then you are not too sure.

Uncle Jack wanted to try something called "escargots" but he didn't know how to say it so he wound up having "prawns" because that was the only thing on the menu he could pronounce.

He enjoyed them even more when he found out what a narrow escape he had with the "escargots." Somebody finally told him what they are but he is not going to tell you what they are because it would make you sick to think that a good restaurant would try to sell you something like that just because you don't know how to speak French.

To give you some idea how good the prawns were, Uncle Jack will tell you they were about half as good as the shrimp Mr. Basil Daniels used to cook when he had his restaurant on the causeway and if you were ever lucky enough to eat his shrimp you will know how good that is. Half as good as that is still pretty good.

Anyway, there is a lot more Uncle Jack would like to tell you about the Europa Hotel, like how he woke up the next morning with chocolate in his ear for example, but he has run out of space.

Night Calls

Dear Uncle Jack,

I read in the *Current* that the Outer Banks Medical Center isn't going to be able to stay open after midnight any more. What should I do if I get really sick at 2 o'clock in the morning, Uncle Jack?

Worried,
Kitty Hawk

Dear Worried,

You could do what Uncle Jack does. Take two aspirins and drink a large Pepsi and watch an old movie on Channel 11. If that doesn't work you can always drive to Norfolk. They have a Peoples Drug Store up there where you can get an Alka-Seltzer any time of the night.

Helpfully,
Uncle Jack

The Year Ahead

Uncle Jack spent a couple of cold January days in bed with the flu last week so he had plenty of time to look ahead (through bloodshot eyes) at what might be in store for the Outer Banks during the coming year.

FEBRUARY: A mild northeaster topples 12 houses into the surf in South Nags Head. Most of the wreckage washes ashore near Salvo where happy developers announce they will use it to build 24 new oceanfront condos.

MARCH: More than 250 Outer Banks restaurants officially open for the season, joining 47 others that pretended to stay open all winter. Of the 250 about 75 are actually new and the others are under new ownership. In their "Grand Opening" advertisements the restauranteurs collectively demonstrated 47 different ways to spell the word "cuisine."

APRIL: Chamber of Commerce officials announce that Easter weekend was the biggest ever on the Outer Banks, drawing an estimated 1.5 million visitors who spent approximately $6.5 million more than last year. An informal survey of area businesses, however, reveals that most businessmen actually made less money this Easter weekend than last. "For the life of us we can't figure out why that is," a Chamber spokesman says.

MAY: Dare County officials predict that the severe labor shortage which has plagued Outer Banks employers for the past several seasons will be worse than ever this summer. Citing the continuing shortage of low-cost housing for seasonal workers, one county commissioner proposes setting aside 40 acres of the Baum Tract in Kill Devil Hills as a designated overnight parking area where workers and their Labrador retrievers could sleep in their pickup trucks without fear of hassling by local police. "They could use the toilets over at the new Chamber of Commerce building, so it wouldn't cost the county a cent," the commissioner suggests.

JUNE: A spokesman for Global International Malls of Lausanne, Switzerland, announces that his company will seek rezoning of a 400-acre tract fronting the Bypass in Kill Devil Hills. "We are confident the town fathers will want to approve the rezoning," spokesman Jim Bob Tacky says, "when they learn that our new shopping center will employ up to 35 persons, at least during July and August." He adds that Global International will present each commissioner with a Gucci bag filled with unmarked twenties, "no strings attached," as soon as the rezoning has been effected.

JULY: An overloaded tractor-trailer overturns while attempting to negotiate the sharp curve in front of the Duck Deli, dumping 18 tons of bamboo shingles onto the narrow roadway and bringing traffic to a standstill from Wilmington, N.C., to Wilmington, Del. "They have got to do something about this bleeping road," says truck driver Byron Munschausen of Raleigh, who was attempting to deliver things to the Casa del Sushi development north of Corolla where 780 bamboo and stucco townhouses are under construction. Munschausen speaks highly of the hot pastrami with Swiss on rye at the Duck Deli where he dines for several days while waiting for his employers to fly in a laborer to reload his truck.

AUGUST: Currituck County commissioners give the go-ahead to Consolidated Intergalactic Land Co. of Rocky Mount for "Lorna Dunes," a proposed 3,000-unit ocean-to-sound development near the Virginia line. When questioned by taxpayers who complain that the only access road is already seriously overtaxed, that water supplies are inadequate, and power shortages imminent, the commissioners respond in unison, "So?"

SEPTEMBER: The Dare County Tourist Bureau reports that in spite of horrendous traffic jams, overcrowded beaches, poor service in shops and restaurants due to lack of help, and typically lousy summer fishing, more people visited the Outer Banks and spent more money last year than in any previous season. While most visitors appear to have had a good time in spite of all the aggravations, one vacationer, identified as a "Mr. Berra" of New York City, complains that "this place is getting so crowded nobody wants to come here any more." (OBX)

Uncle Jack Knows

Staying Here

Uncle Jack may have mentioned once or twice before how hard it used to be for him to pack up his old red van and drive back to Pittsburgh on Labor Day after a whole summer on the Outer Banks.

He had to do that 12 or 13 times before he finally moved to Nags Head once and for all where he is now living happily ever after and he is getting ready to enjoy another fall season which is surely the best time to be here with the possible exception of winter and spring.

The main thing which made him remember how awful it was to have to leave Nags Head on Labor Day was the weather over this past Labor Day weekend. He is fairly sure that every last one of the 3 million people who were here would agree with him that weatherwise it was just about as perfect as a long weekend could be.

Several times Uncle Jack actually stopped counting his money and went out of his shop and just stood in the parking lot and let the warm sunshine fall directly upon his gray skin and he feels the cool northeast breeze blowing over his withered body and he could tell that fall is just around the corner.

He is not going to say any more about this, though, because he knows it is cruel to tell all the people who are stuck in awful places like Ohio and Louisville how nice it is down here on the Outer Banks right now.

He would just like to thank them all for staying where they are and not aggravating the local water situation any worse than it already is.

(OBX)

Real Nightlife

Dear Uncle Jack,

How's the nightlife on the Outer Banks?

Born to Swing,

Erie, Pennsylvania

Dear Born,

The most prevalent form of nightlife on the Outer Banks is a species of small, translucent crab that emerges on the beach after dark. The best way to observe them is to drive down the beach in your ORV with the headlights on and watch them scamper to avoid being crushed.

Crabbily,

Uncle Jack

Fall, the True Prime Season[*]

Boomer asked Uncle Jack to write a short piece about fall on the Outer Banks, which he is happy to do because it is a subject dear to his heart. He has spent all or part of every fall for the past 40 years on the Outer Banks, and he can tell you there is no place on earth he would rather be when the summer madness subsides after Labor Day.

It is in the fall when Uncle Jack is most grateful for the schools that incarcerate great numbers of children from September on, effectively preventing their parents from vacationing on the Outer Banks during what should really be the prime season for tourists and locals alike. Thanks to the schools, the vast majority of potential visitors are forced to take their vacations in July and August, the two most miserable months of the year in terms of heat and humidity, and the resulting crowds and insane traffic have made summer on the Outer Banks the dreadful

[*] *Boomer* magazine, Oct.-Nov. 2012. Reprinted with permission.

scene it has become in recent years.

Uncle Jack loves fall for all the obvious reasons: the cooler and drier air, the relatively uncrowded beaches, restaurants and shops, and the slightly less lunatic traffic on major roads like the hilariously misnamed "Bypass" through Kitty Hawk, Kill Devil Hills and Nags Head, which has claimed more lives this year than Mother Nature's dreaded rip tides.

He knows that some folks feel that winter is the best season of all because of the even greater absence of people and traffic, but he has found that winter also has some serious drawbacks. After coping with frozen pipes and icy northeast winds for a couple of years, he decided that winter on the Outer Banks could be paradise only for confirmed masochists, so he began to flee to cozier places like New Orleans for a couple of months after Christmas. He believes that if the Tourist Bureau ever succeeds in building a convention center in Nags Head, they would have no trouble persuading the Masochist's Society to hold its annual meeting there in February when they could enjoy unique and pleasurable romps like climbing Jockey's Ridge in the nude during northeasters.

There was a time in the old days when the fantastic fishing was what Uncle Jack most loved about fall on the Outer Banks. Those were the days when huge schools of enormous bluefish would chase smaller fish into the surf where crowds of equally rapacious fishermen (including Uncle Jack) awaited what was often a once-in-a-lifetime opportunity to live out their wildest fishing fantasies. Every cast of a shiny Hopkins lure (or even a rusty bottle opener) would bring a ferocious bite and, barring a broken line, the successful landing of a monster blue. Hundreds would be caught in the space of an hour, not a few of which would wind up rotting on the beach, much as buffalo did in another place and time. Uncle Jack hasn't seen or heard of a monster "bluefish blitz" on the Outer Banks, for many years, so perhaps the blues did go the way of the buffalo. Or maybe they just decided to go somewhere less dangerous to feed.

Finally, Uncle Jack must confess that another aspect of fall on the Outer Banks that he greatly enjoyed is the storms. He never hopes for storms because he knows from firsthand experience that they can do tremendous damage and even kill people. But he also knows they are inevitable on the Outer Banks and that being in the middle of one can be about as exciting as life can get.

He first learned this from a hurricane named Ginger over 40 years ago when she came calling during his first fall on the Outer Banks. She wasn't much as hurricanes go, but Uncle Jack was quite sure at 3 a.m. on October 1, 1971, that she was about to blow his house down and that he and his family were doomed. It's a fascinating story involving the emptying of Roanoke Sound and the discovery of a wrecked WWII airplane out in back of his house but it will have to wait for another time.**

Over the years he has rubbed elbows with other windy visitors with names like Gloria and Emily and Dennis and Floyd and Isabel and Irene, who collectively drowned three of his cars and ripped the roof off his framing shop twice.

But he has forgiven them all because they were, after all, inescapable and unforgettable aspects of Uncle Jack's favorite season on the Outer Banks, the fall.

** NOTE: Jack elaborates now, for this book: "The hurricane blew all the water out of the sound in back of my house. Some oceanfront friends had been blown out of their house during the night and came to camp out with us. At first light their intrepid ten-year-old son walked out into the fog-shrouded sound by himself and returned in a half-hour dragging a rather heavy anchor through the mud. He told us to follow his footsteps a short distance and said that we would find the wreckage of an airplane, which we did. Part of the tail and propeller and engine were sticking up through the mud draped with fragments of fishermen's nets. We broke off a piece of what might have been landing gear and dragged it back to the house where it sat for many years until it rusted away to nothing by our back steps. We learned later that a WWII training plane had crashed into the sound at some point and the pilot's body had been found floating near Colington Island but the plane had not been found. The stainless steel anchor became the anchor for a 17-foot runabout I owned for a few years back in the '80s. That's my story and I'm stickin' to it."

Erosion and Politics

Dear Uncle Jack,

How about that crazy ocean last week? Seriously, Uncle Jack, what are we going to do about the erosion around here? You must have learned a lot about erosion in high school science class, so let's hear it.

Bobby Bulkhead
Kill Devil Hills

Dear Bobby,

You are right that Uncle Jack knows a fair amount about erosion but he sure didn't learn about it in high school science. Up in northern Wisconsin where he went to high school there was not very much erosion going on so the teacher did not spend a whole lot of time on it. Instead Uncle Jack learned a lot about ice and snow and sleet and how to breathe when it is 40 degrees below zero, and a lot of that knowledge really comes in handy when he is down under the house fixing his frozen pipes, too.

If you want to know the truth he did not learn anything about erosion until he moved to Virginia Beach about 30 years ago and he asked somebody about all those big pipes they have on the beach which you have to climb over to get to the ocean. It turned out that the big pipes

were there to pump sand back on the the beach after it
washed away every winter and that was when he started
learning about erosion. Those big pipes are still there, too,
and they keep pumping sand like crazy and they haul it on
trucks, too, but every year the beach gets a little smaller.

Anyway he found out that erosion is not hard to
understand because it is just sand getting pushed around
by the ocean just the way it has for millions of years. If you
want to know the truth erosion was a pretty boring subject
until people started putting buildings on top of sand that
the ocean wasn't through moving yet, and now erosion is
very interesting to a lot of people and especially the ones
who own those buildings.

If you ask Uncle Jack, though, erosion is not half
as interesting as what you could call the "politics of erosion." And the more he learns about the politics of erosion
the more confused he gets.

First he read in the paper where the state legisla-
ture passed this law called the Coastal Area Management
Act which was supposed to make it harder for people to do
dumb things like putting buildings too close to the ocean.
Uncle Jack thought that sounded like a pretty good law but
then he read in the paper that if you do go ahead and build
too close to the ocean you can go to the federal government and get cheap insurance to cover your building when
it falls into the ocean. You can probably understand why he
would be a little confused about that.

Anyway the next thing he read in the paper was that
this N.C. agency called the Coastal Resources Commission
had come up with a new rule which says that if you want to
build a big building near the ocean you have to put it back
far enough so it won't be washed away for several years.

Uncle Jack thought that was a very smart thing to do because he knew how much trouble the big buildings caused for Virginia Beach. But then he read in the paper that the new rule made the county commissioners very mad and they told the Coastal Resources Commission to go away and leave Dare County alone, so then he didn't know what to think.

Then just last week he read in the paper that the county commissioners were feeling better again because some high official of the Coastal Resources Commission came to Dare County to look at some big buildings that are so close to the ocean that sometimes they are in the ocean depending on which way the wind is blowing.

The official said he was going to do everything he could to protect those buildings which never would have been built where they are if the new rule which the county commissioners don't like had been in effect when the new buildings were built.

So you can see why Uncle Jack gets confused sometimes about the politics of erosion.

Anyway he does feel sorry for all the people who built their houses in the wrong place and he hopes they can find some good way to save them. But he also hopes that one mistake will not lead to another the way it did up in Massachusetts and New Jersey where a lot of towns managed to save their big buildings but lost their beach in the process.

This is a very hard problem and Uncle Jack needs to lie down and think about it some more so that is what he is going to do. Right now.

Thoughtfully,
Uncle Jack

Corolla
Odyssey

The sad death of the colt that was killed by a car on the beach near Corolla a couple of weeks ago has reminded Uncle Jack how lucky he was to experience that wonderful ride up the beach from Corolla to the Virginia line before progress set in up there.

He realizes he was a Johnny-come-lately compared to his friend Everett Tate who was born and raised up there way back when car was synonymous with Model T and very few folks around here could afford to own one. But everything is relative, as Einstein said, so Uncle Jack is going to do some reminiscing just like he was a genuine old-timer.

If you would prefer to hear from a genuine, genuine old-timer you could talk to Everett, or better yet, to his mother who is in her nineties and still lives in the house in which she was born in Duck. (It's the little house surrounded by drooling developers.)

Anyway the first time Uncle Jack made that

magical trip up the beach was back in 1969 with a friend in his ancient Land Rover, the 4-wheel drive capability of which was tested long before they got to Corolla.

The wind was out of the northwest that day and the road along the sound where the Barrier Island Restaurant is today had vanished as it often did in those days and occasionally does even today.

There was no Barrier Island Restaurant, of course, and the words "condo" and "timeshare" were as exotic as Dar es Salaam and Timbuktu. There were sanderlings everywhere but no Sanderling, pines but no Pine Island, Corolla lighthouse but not Corolla Light.

Most of the land between Duck and Corolla was as empty as it was when it was a bombing range during WWII. For a long time one of Uncle Jack's most treasured possessions was an unexploded rocket he found along the road north of Duck, many more of which no doubt lurk beneath the surface of various upscale subdivisions along there along with God knows what other military detritus.

After loading up at the Corolla store with Moon Pies, Nabs, Snickers, Lance crackers, Cokes, potato chips and the like (in quantities sufficient to survive being stuck in the sand for two or three days—which, of course, never happened but at least Uncle Jack was prepared) the Land Rover crawled eastward over the dunes and onto the incredibly wide flat beach in front of the lighthouse.

From there to the Virginia line on a weekday you could drive for miles without seeing another car, much less a building supply truck. Here and there you saw a rusting travel trailer up on blocks, wild horses grazing in the dunes, maybe one of Ernie Bowden's exotic beasties wallowing in the surf, cooling its extremities while trying to escape the voracious black flies.

Uncle Jack will never forget the first time he saw the stumps at Wash Woods, poking up everywhere on the beach and well out into the ocean. There were hundreds of them that day—perhaps thousands on another day when he made the same trek right after the Halloween Storm of 1991.

Any doubter who is reluctant to believe that the beaches ain't where they used to be would have a hard time explaining Wash Woods.

Uncle Jack has made that once awe-inspiring trek perhaps a dozen times since 1969, each time with less enjoyment as the traffic worsened and that which was once pleasurable became nerve-wracking.

It came as no surprise to him that a horse had been run over on the beach last month. After his last trip a few years ago he wonders how it is possible that no human lives have been lost in the craziness that prevails up there these days, especially on weekends when the Tidewater cowboys come down in their jacked-up 4WDs and play like Richard Petty at Daytona Beach.

It was fun while it lasted.

Natives and Locals

Dear Uncle Jack,

On the Outer Banks, what's the difference between a "native" and a local"?

Tourist
Pittsburgh

Dear Tourist,

A local is somebody who lives here all year round but isn't a native. Most locals used to live in or near Pittsburgh. Locals are permitted to leave the Outer Banks for up to three weeks during January or February. If they stay away longer, they are shunned by other locals who sneer at them and call them tourists.

A native is somebody whose family has always lived here. Natives never leave the Outer Banks except to join the Coast Guard.

Natives converse with each other in an unintelligible tongue which many linguists believe to be an early form of English. Many natives carry on the ancient trades and crafts of their forefathers such as hunting, fishing, crabbing and selling real estate.

As far as Uncle Jack has been able to determine, there are no anatomical differences between natives and locals that would prevent them from mating.

Insouciantly,
Uncle Jack

The Adventures of Uncle Jack

Uncle Jack
Gets a Laptop

ACT 1: TAKING THE LAPTOP LEAP

Poor Gary Kasparov is not the only one who has tangled with computers lately. Uncle Jack has decided to join the 20th century before it is too late by acquiring a real computer with which he can hook up to the Internet and do amazing things like write letters to his grandchildren electronically at about a hundred times the cost of regular mail.

He decided to get what they call a "laptop" computer because one of the main features of a laptop is that you can haul it around where you go such as out on the deck or into the living room where your barcalounger is located or into the bedroom if you are too lazy to sit in your barcalounger.

That was the easiest decision he had to make, though, because he found out there are about 200 laptop computers out there in the marketplace and they are all wonderful for various reasons, none of which Uncle Jack is capable of comprehending.

Little did he know, for example, that some laptops have 16 megabytes of RAM while others have only 8 or even 4. He has no idea what a megabyte is but more is better, apparently, which is not true of everything such as children. Nor did he know that all laptops have "hard drives" whose prowess is measured in "gigabytes" which is even better than megabytes for many purposes.

He now knows that some laptops have "floppy disks" and some have CD-ROMs and some have both and he is confident that one day he will know what they are and why they are so important.

In the meantime he is reading everything he can get his hands on about laptop computers, much of which consists of sentences like these:

> The DTK notebook uses a UMC chip set, 256K of synchronous L2 cache, and EDO DRAM.

> The 133-MHz CD PowerBrick had low benchmark test scores compared with similar machines, but a 12.1-inch active-matrix display, a 1.3GB Toshiba hard disk, a four-year warranty, and a bundled 28.8/14.4-Kbps fax modem tip the scales back in its favor.

Uncle Jack prides himself on being a high school graduate but he has to confess that his confidence has been shaken somewhat by his first encounters with "computertalk." Reading William Faulkner in Urdu would be a snap compared to what he has plowed through in the last couple of weeks. But he did finally make a decision about which laptop to buy.

He has ordered a Gateway Solo 2100 which as far as he can tell has plenty of megabytes and giga-bytes and hard drives and both a floppy disk and a CD-ROM and numerous other features that might come in handy when he writes to his grandchildren such as a modem which takes the place of a stamped envelope and only costs $110.

The main reason he bought a Gateway, though, is because he could sit in his barcalounger and order it over the phone instead of driving to Virginia Beach to get it. They told him they would send it as soon as the snow melts up in South Dakota and UPS trucks can get to the factory which could be any week now.

Uncle Jack has a sinking feeling that his life will never be the same. Pandora never knew what hit her either.

ACT 2: TO BOLDLY GO ...

Uncle Jack is pleased to report that this is the very first column he has written with the aid, if that is the right word (he could have chiseled this on stone in half the time), of his brand new state-of-the-art Gate-way Solo 2100 Multimedia Notebook, also known as his *&%#@! laptop. Actually, he should say that this is the first paragraph he has written on his new laptop because he is not at all sure that he will make it to the end without doing something inadvertently that will cause the screen to go blank. Also, he has no confi-dence that once he gets far enough to "save" what he has written that he will not lose it forever somewhere in the electronic labyrinth.

Nevertheless, he is determined to persist and

eventually prevail over this incredible machine which he knows he will never understand but which he thinks might be both useful and fun in the long run (assuming they will let him use it in the old folks home or the loony bin, whichever comes first).

He can tell you that nothing is simple with the sole exception of pushing the "on" button which you would think would also be the "off" button but this is not the case. He is not going to try to explain what you have to go through to turn the thing off but he can tell you that if Lincoln had written the Gettysburg Address on Uncle Jack's Laptop he never would have gotten to the cemetery in time to deliver it.

As of this writing Uncle Jack has not yet found his way to the Internet which was the main reason for getting his laptop in the first place. (He has hallucinations about becoming a major player in the lucrative world of online antique print and map sales.) Today as he hunts and pecks he is waiting for the Sprint man to come and install a second telephone line for his laptop which he has discovered he desperately needs, mainly because he cannot be on the Internet and talk with the Gateway Computer Company's technical support staff out in South Dakota at the same time. This is one of the many hidden costs of doing business on the Internet and he is sure he will discover many more before he makes his first dime, if he ever does.

So far Uncle Jack has spent perhaps four hours on the phone with three different Gateway technicians who have, with infinite patience, helped him track down and eliminate a bewildering variety of glitches including pollution of the hard drive which is a condition he urges you to avoid at all cost. While these technicians all sounded like they had escaped from the cast of Fargo, he can tell you they know their stuff by golly.

He has to confess that notwithstanding all the frustrations and aggravations of the first couple of weeks with his new laptop, he really loves it. For years he has been saying to all who would listen that computers are not for Uncle Jack—not while there are books to read and beaches to walk on. You'll never find him sitting for hours in a stuffy room, pushing a little arrow around a screen; that's for nerds who can find nothing better to do with their precious time on earth. Bill Gates will never see a dime of Uncle Jack's hard-earned money. That's what he said and it was all a lie. He is hooked.

See you on the 'net, folks. Watch for Uncle Jack's Web Page—coming soon to your screen.

ACT 3: DIGITAL BRAIN SURGERY

Uncle Jack's tortuous journey through cyberspace ended abruptly this week. Last Sunday morning his laptop refused to "boot up" in the normal fashion when he turned it on and after two hours of diagnostic probing by phone the computer doctor in South Dakota decided that a serious operation was needed. Uncle Jack's laptop would have to have its "hard drive" replaced immediately.

The doctor explained that this was roughly equivalent to a brain replacement in a human being and that his laptop would remember nothing after the operation. It would not remember any of the email letters from potential customers all over the globe. It would remember none of the dozens of email addresses in Uncle Jack's electronic address book. It would remember none of the programs Uncle Jack has installed over the past few weeks to operate his modem, his printer, his scanner and God knows what else.

When he installs his new hard drive next week Uncle Jack will resume his voyage through cyberspace from the digital equivalent of square one. Incurable optimist that he is, Uncle Jack had saved nothing onto floppy disks, a simple procedure that would have saved him hours of tedious work in days to come—a mistake he will not make again.

There was a time when Uncle Jack would have greeted this dreadful news with all manner of ranting and raving and carrying on over the unfairness of it all and he would be unfit for normal social intercourse for days. His children would have cowered in their rooms and his cats and dogs would have gone to live with the neighbors.

He is pleased to report that this is no longer the case. He is not happy about this unfortunate development but neither is he despairing. Being told that his hard drives needs to be replaced is not the same as being told that he has inoperable cancer of the goiter or that one of his granddaughters has eloped with a lawyer. In other words Uncle Jack has at last achieved a healthy perspective on life that allows him to distinguish between the trivial and the important.

And not a moment too soon, either, his loved ones will tell you.

(OBX)

 The
Demon Sex

Dear Uncle Jack,

I have been reading a lot in the papers lately about how the Town of Nags Head is agonizing over what to do about dirty movies and topless bars and other sordid things like that which are threatening our way of life here on the Outer Banks. You live in Nags Head, Uncle Jack, so what do you think they ought to do?

Kari Nation
Wanchese

Dear Kari,

This is not a subject that Uncle Jack spends a whole lot of time worrying about but he has a few thoughts that he will be happy to share with you since you asked.

For one thing he knows that people have been trying to deal with the Demon Sex for a very long time— even before there was a Bible to provide them with clear guidelines. You may not believe this but anthropologists have discovered that there were harlots roaming the earth, leading men astray, as early as the Fifth Century B.C.

Down through the centuries the good people have been trying every which way to stamp out the evil manifestations of the Demon Sex (along with his cousins the Demon Rum and the Demon Dope) but he has to be honest and tell you that it does not look like they have made very much progress so far.

It has gotten so bad that if Uncle Jack's flesh was any weaker he would be inclined to throw in the towel and let the bad people have their way with him.

But Uncle Jack remains strong in his resolve and he believes that the only way to turn the tide against the Demon Sex is to crack down even harder on his handy-men (and handywomen).

To this end he suggests that during the off-season when the town police are not so busy writing speeding tickets they should go to work rounding up the bad people such as the harlots and the men who consort with them and the people who traffic in dirty movies and the people who watch them and they should be stripped naked and tied to a stake in front of the Nags Head Town Hall (it is not too late to add a stake to the new complex and it should not push the project over budget if the commissioners don't get conned into buying a fancy rhinestone stake from Tammi Bakker or somebody like that).

Then they should schedule regular public whip-pings and invite the mayors of all the towns and maybe other celebrities such as Pat Buchanan or Pat Robertson to do the honors.

Uncle Jack is fairly confident that a spectacle of this nature would draw a good crowd and would go a long way toward stamping out the Demon Sex in our communities. Whether or not parents should bring their children would be up to them but if they decide to leave them home they should be aware of what they might be watching on TV.

Anyway, there is a lot more Uncle Jack could say on this subject but he has run out of space and he is probably in big enough trouble already so he is going to stop right here.

Prudently,
Uncle Jack

Winnebago Blues

Dear Uncle Jack,

One night last week I was racing up the Bypass to get some cough medicine for my baby but I got behind this big Winnebago with Kansas plates going 25 mph and by the time got past them it was too late. The ABC store was closed so I had to turn around and go back to South Nags Head and explain to my baby why I couldn't get her cough medicine and she got sore and made the kids go to bed instead of watching *Jeopardy* and she pulled the plug on me, too, if you know what I mean.

Needless to say I'm disgusted and the reason I am telling you all this, Uncle Jack, is that I know you are the kind of person who has to get to the ABC store in a big hurry yourself sometimes so you know how I feel. I thought maybe if you published this letter it would galvanize lawmakers into action to do something about all the slow drivers on the Bypass. I think they should pass a law that would make it a felony not to drive as fast as the law allows at all times.

Junior Johnson
South Nags Head

Dear Junior,

Uncle Jack knows exactly how you feel. He, too, has spent many an hour creeping along behind large recreational vehicles on the Bypass and wondering if he would ever get where he is going which is usually but not always the ABC store. He has to confess he does enjoy reading all those stickers they put on the back of those RVs but he wonders sometimes how you could get to all those scenic and historical places such as Knott's Berry Farm and Tarpon World all in one lifetime if you never drove over 25 mph.

He is sorry to tell you he does not think there is much the lawmakers can do about this problem so from now on maybe you should do what Uncle Jack does and plan ahead so you do not have to make so many emergency trips to the ABC store. One way to do this is to take out a home equity loan and stock up on whatever you think you will need between now and the end of the tourist season. Uncle Jack is pretty sure you can deduct the interest from your income tax so that makes it a pretty good deal if you are careful not to lose your house.

On the other hand if you live in South Nags Head you are probably going to lose your house sooner or later anyway so it might not make any difference.

Uncle Jack does not think it would be a good idea to make those Winnebagos go faster because if you ask him the only thing worse than being behind a large RV going 25 mph is to be in front of one when it is going more than 25 mph. Anyway Uncle Jack knows that all those slow-moving people with the funny license plates are the ones who make it possible for him to live on the Outer Banks all the time instead of just visiting once in a while so he is willing to put up with a slow trip to the ABC store once in a while.

Diplomatically,
Uncle Jack

Flea Doctor

Dear Uncle Jack,

This is a hard letter for me to write because I have a problem that is so embarrassing I can hardly talk about it. Before I tell you what my problem is I want to assure you that I am not the kind of person you would expect to have a problem like this. Up in Scranton, Pa., where I used to live before my husband dragged me down here to the Outer Banks to live, I was noted for the exceptional cleanliness of my house so my personal hygiene habits are above reproach.

In short, I am a clean person in every way, Uncle Jack, and this is why I am ashamed to tell you about my problem. I am desperate, though, so I am going to tell you. I have fleas in my house.

The fleas are making life miserable for both Fred and myself. It is not even flea season yet and already my ankles look like chopped liver and poor Fred is in even worse shape. I should tell you that Fred is my dog, not my husband. (Arthur is my husband and he makes life miserable for Fred and me, too, but that is another story which I will tell you about some other time.)

As I was saying, I am desperate. I have tried every flea remedy in the book but nothing seems to work.

Anyway, I am at the end of my rope, Uncle Jack, and writing to you is the last resort of a truly desperate person. They told me over at the laundromat that you are one of those people who thinks he knows everything about everything so let's have it. Personally I think I am probably wasting a stamp but as I say, I am desperate.

Tormented,
Kill Devil Hills

Dear Tormented,

Uncle Jack is very glad you brought this shameful problem to him because he is quite sure he can help you. He has to tell you, though, that he is slightly peeved by your attitude. You make it sound like Uncle Jack is some kind of know-it-all who gets a big kick out of flaunting his vast knowledge in front of ordinary persons such as yourself.

Well he will tell you that nothing could be further from the truth. Uncle Jack did not seek the mantle of greatness; it was thrust upon him by fate. He tries his best to use his great powers of intellect to help other people but there are many times he wishes he was just an ordinary stupid person like everybody else.

Anyway, Uncle Jack forgives you because he knows from personal experience the depths of the agony to which you have sunk. Thanks to his old dog Ralph, who has been a walking blood bank for fleas ever since he moved to the Outer Banks, Uncle Jack has known the torment of which you speak so eloquently. But no more! Both Uncle Jack and Ralph have been almost flea-free for nearly six weeks now thanks to a new treatment Ralph received from his personal physician at the dog clinic in Kitty Hawk. He can tell you the treatment consists of a foul-smelling liquid applied in drops to Ralph's exterior, from which the fleas depart as though he was the Titanic going down for the last time. He is happy to tell you that the horrible smell goes away after only a few days.

Uncle Jack does not know if this treatment will work on every dog but he can tell you it has given Ralph and him new leases on life and maybe it can do the same for you and Fred.

Now what was it you wanted to tell Uncle Jack about your husband?

Helpfully,
Uncle Jack

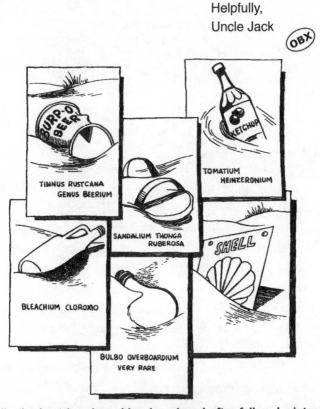

While the best beachcombing is enjoyed after fall and winter storms that litter the sand with shells and other delightful dredgings from the sea bottom, there is much for the summer treasure hunter to seek as well. The items pictured above were found on the beach in Nags Head during the summer of 1981. (Photo courtesy N.C. Marine Resources Center, Manteo)

The
Vanishing
Hotels

Uncle Jack has been reading a lot in the papers this week about Nags Head's vanishing hotels and motels and the proposals that have been made to "turn the tide"—if that is the right expression—and get developers to build more hotels instead of tearing them down. According to Nags Head officials, some 13 hotels and motels have been demolished since 1999.

But the process began long before that as many will remember:

THE OLD NAGSHEADER with its glorious wraparound porches stood proudly for more than 40 years at the 11 milepost on the Beach Road until it burned to the ground in a spectacular blaze in the fall of 1977. It nearly took Uncle Jack's then brand-new Yellowhouse Gallery with it when the wind switched and blew burning embers onto its cedar shake roof.

The fire was mysterious to say the least and was generally believed to be deliberately set to remove the beautiful but no longer economically viable building from an oceanfront tract that would eventually sprout a half-dozen of the large houses that have become the new Nags Head vernacular. As far as Uncle Jack can remember, it was the first hotel to be destroyed deliberately for that purpose. (The magnificent old ARLINGTON HOTEL had preceded it in death by several years but at the merciless hands of Mother Nature.)

The old HOLLOWELL HOTEL on the west side of the Beach Road in the "historic district" had fallen to the wreckers even earlier but the lot on which it stood is still vacant. Uncle Jack had once eyed it as a possible future location for his gallery (then at the First Colony Inn) but when it sold at auction (along with a very large lot stretching to the Bypass) for a little over $20,000 he was too poor to bid. Sigh.

The Hollowell Hotel had been moved over from its original location on the sound after the Beach Road was built in 1930, but it lacked many of the amenities picky northern tourists had come to demand, such as running water and electricity, so it went into decline. At the end, it was a defunct store from which Mr. Hollowell himself sold off the furnishings, one of which was a homemade counter which Uncle Jack bought for $1.00 (he could afford that) which now serves as the front desk at Yellow-house Gallery—a tremendous link with the past.

He has fond memories of the original NAGS HEAD INN, too. When he was managing First Colony Inn at its original location on the oceanfront back in 1970, he was sometimes able to direct desperate tourists to it when they arrived in Nags Head in peak season without a reservation. It was about the most wretched accommodation on the entire Outer Banks at that time and would always be the last to fill up—often with low-end bikers who were even less fussy about the rooms than the owners were about their clientele.

The old Nags Head Inn was just a memory in 1985 when the sparkling oceanfront edifice bearing its name went up. Uncle Jack remembers the opening very well because he and his redoubtable framer, Tom Tully, had cranked out some 280 pictures to hang on the walls of what would become the first, and until now the last, large modern hotel in town. (They won't be doing that again.)

The pace of destruction has definitely picked up in recent years. When he left for London on Oct. 1, the CABANA EAST, once part of the late George Crocker's empire, was still standing where it had been for at least the past 35 years, across the street from the long-departed Galleon Esplanade which has been replaced by you-know-what. When Uncle Jack returned four weeks later, the Cabana East was gone and four sets of pilings stood in its place, ready to support new McMansions.

Before that, the OLDE LONDON INN, the VIVIANNA, the TARHEEL, the CAROLINIAN and too many more to remember disappeared. Part of the WHALEBONE in South Nags Head was carted off to the landfill last week after Isabel did to it in a few hours what it would have taken an army of UVA students on Spring Break a week to accomplish.

Several miles north the venerable Sea Spray is shuttered while it awaits demolition. Both the Sea Oatel and the Sea Foam near Whalebone Junction narrowly escaped Isabel but the future for both seems fraught with peril.

So where does Nags Head go from here, hotel-wise? Uncle Jack fervently hopes that all concerned will recognize the folly of building large new hotels, or any other immovable buildings, on the oceanfront. Mother Nature is clearly winning the Battle of the Beaches, and there isn't enough money in the world, much less Washington, to stop her.

Sign of the Times

Dear Uncle Jack,

  I read in the paper where one of the billboard companies wants to put a big billboard on one of those marshy islands over by the causeway in Nags Head. The paper said the Nags Head commissioners were pretty upset about that and so were the Dare County commissioners—except for the one who sold the island to the billboard company so they could put a sign on it.

  Anyway, I would like to know what you think about putting a sign on that island and also who you are mad at if anybody.

Sammy Otica
Drainfield

Dear Sammy,

  Uncle Jack was very interested when he read that article in the paper because he can see that little island from his back porch without even getting up out of his rocking chair. If you want to know the truth he was somewhat relieved when he read about the billboard because he has been wondering how long it would take for some developer to figure out a way to build a 24-unit condominium on that island which is sometimes a full four inches above sea level depending on which way the wind is blowing so it is fair game. Anyway when you think about what else they could have built over there such as a major theme park a billboard does not sound too bad.

Uncle Jack is the kind of person who tries to look on the bright side of every ecological disaster so he has been working overtime trying to think of some good points about putting a large billboard out there in Roanoke Sound. For one thing they have a lot of swanky restaurants around there where the tourists like to sit and watch the sunsets while they are eating. Uncle Jack knows that most of those sunsets are so terrific they can almost take your mind off how much you are paying for your dinner.

Sometimes, though, the sunsets are fairly puny and not much better than what you would see up in Ohio or Pennsylvania or any other place where the tourists come from so that is when a nice big billboard would come in handy out there. For example Uncle Jack has seen some terrific billboards where the Marlboro Man is sitting on his horse and the sun is going down behind them and it is very beautiful to look at. Maybe they could get the Marlboro company to make a billboard where the Marlboro man is holding up a big bluefish he just caught which would give it more of a local flavor.

Also the way modern technology is going these days maybe they could get some Japanese company to put a large-screen TV out there with a videotape of a beautiful sunset and run commercials over the top of it the way they do on the Weather Channel. That way the local shopkeepers like Uncle Jack who do not get to eat dinner until after dark could also enjoy a nice sunset once in a while during the tourist season.

Anyway, the paper said they are going to build a two-faced sign out there and it seems to Uncle Jack that a two-faced sign is exactly what they ought to build when you consider which commissioner's idea this was in the first place.

> Resignedly,
> Uncle Jack

Happy New Year

Dear Uncle Jack,

Well, it's a brand new year on the Outer Banks and elsewhere. I would like to know if you are making any resolutions or predictions and if so what they are so we can look back a year from now and see how stupid they were.

> Avid Reader
> Stumpy Point

Dear Avid,

And a Happy New Year to you, too. Uncle Jack appreciates your expression of support as he makes his annual attempt to improve himself and also to prognosticate what the future may bring to his fellow residents of the Outer Banks so they may better prepare themselves for any eventuality.

He would be the first to admit that he has not done too well in either department in recent years but he is not the kind of person who gives up easily in the face of adversity.

Uncle Jack this year has made a resolution that he is pretty sure he can keep no matter what, to wit: he is going to stay in New Orleans until April no matter how homesick he gets for the Outer Banks.

When he sees on the Weather Channel how a humongous northeaster is pounding the Outer Banks and he wants desperately to be there to see his neighbors' houses in South Nags Head fall into the ocean, he will remember his resolution and he will stay put in New Orleans no matter how warm and pleasant and boring it is. Unless, of course, his money runs out which is always a possibility when you are a big tipper like Uncle Jack.

If you want to know the truth Uncle Jack has not been very much better at making predictions than he has at keeping resolutions.

Each year for a long time he has been predicting that during the coming year another sizeable chunk of the "goodliest land under the cope of heaven" will disappear under a layer of newly laid asphalt and he has been right every time. The fact that your average high school dropout could make the same prediction keeps him from feeling too smug.

One of these years Uncle Jack's prediction is going to be wrong, though, because Mother Nature will decide it's time to do some serious unpaving but neither he nor any other prophet of doom is smart enough to know which year it will be.

Let's all hope it won't be this year. The stockmarket crash will be bad enough.

Prophetically,
Uncle Jack

Curious swimmers examine commercial fisherman Hezekiah Prawn's net shortly after it was hauled from the surf in South Nags Head. Contents included 12 sand sharks, four stingrays, three horseshoe crabs, 17 stinging nettles and a broken vodka bottle—a typical haul for this time of the year according to Mr. Prawn. (Photo by A. Clark Brown.)

Uncle Jack Knows

Watching the Fishermen

Last week's surf-fishing tournament was the first one Uncle Jack ever observed firsthand. He used to read about them in Pittsburgh, and that was better than nothing, but it sure isn't as much fun as the real thing.

For one thing Uncle Jack had absolutely no idea about the amount of beer those fishermen do away with in the course of a tournament. It's like three days of Miller Time.

Now this is Uncle Jack's kind of competitive athletic event. After watching for a few hours he is convinced that by next year he'll be ready to join a team.

Actually Uncle Jack is already an expert in some of the basic skills of competitive surf-fishing:

- He can get out of bed at 8 a.m. and drag himself up to the beach no matter how bad his hangover is;

• He can open a beer with one hand while slicing mullet with the other;

• He can bait his hooks even when his hands are shaking so bad he can't get the cooler open; and

• He can drink six beers before lunch and still locate the Atlantic Ocean without any difficulty.

All Uncle Jack has to do now is learn something about fishing and he could be a real asset to somebody's team. For one thing he hasn't lived down here long enough to have his driver's license revoked so at least he could serve as team chauffeur.

Uncle Jack has already started practicing his fishing skills and he's getting better all the time. Last Sunday morning, for example, he lost three bottom rigs in one hour and caught no fish of any description. This Sunday he lost only one bottom rig and caught two spot. That ought to show that Uncle Jack is a fast learner.

By next October he should be the Compleat Surf Fisherman, able to drink enough beer to float the Crystal Dawn while hauling mackerel two at a time with one hand.

Uncle Jack is already looking forward to next year's tournament. He will start his bladder-stretching exercises in August and when the time comes he will be ready.

Fishing
the Point

Last Sunday was one of those days Uncle Jack used to dream about back when his body was living in Pittsburgh but his mind was on the Outer Banks. It was warm but not too warm and the sun was shining the way it only shines on the Outer Banks and it was his day off so naturally he felt this powerful urge to go fishing.

He went down to the garage and fished his trusty $4.95 Gaylord Perry signature reel out of the bucket of WD-40 where he keeps it between fishing trips and screwed it onto his trusty Junior Johnson signature flounder rod and headed for the beach in his (t)rusty new secondhand Jeep on which he has eight payments to go before he will own what is left of it outright.

He used his time-tested fishing strategy which is where he drives down the beach until he comes to somebody who is catching fish which is where he stops and tries to bum enough bait so he can fish there too. This is a very good plan as long as somebody somewhere is catching fish but if you want to know the truth he drove from one end of Nags Head to the other and he only saw one man fishing and he was not catching anything.

Uncle Jack is not sure where all the fishermen

were but he would not be surprised if they were all sitting in dark rooms somewhere watching the Steelers and Redskins which is a fairly dumb thing to do on a nice Sunday afternoon but he has done it enough times himself so he is not entitled to cast aspersions.

Anyway this lone fisherman mumbled something about how he caught a hundred flounders down at Cape Point the day before and Uncle Jack is the kind of fool who believes stuff like that so he drove right straight down there. He was very lucky to find a good parking place only about a half a mile from the point so he could walk over there and watch all the crazy people standing up to their armpits in freezing water and fishing like there was no tomorrow which is probably close to the truth if what you have to do tomorrow is pack up and drive back to New Jersey.

Anyway he watched for a long time and the only person who caught anything at all was a small boy who snagged a broken conch shell with his Hopkins. Needless to say Uncle Jack did not even bother to bait his hooks and bye and bye he decided to head on over to Bubba's Barbecue and pick up a slab of ribs for dinner which he can tell you is not a bad substitute for flounder when you are in a pinch.

You can imagine how a sensitive person like Uncle Jack must have felt when he turned the key of his new secondhand Jeep and all he heard was a puny little buzzing noise instead of the full-throated roar of his powerful gas-guzzling engine. His worst nightmare had finally happened—his Jeep was dead in the sand at Cape Point and he didn't know how to fix it.

Lucky for him, though, a lot of fishermen

who did not have anything better to do, such as catch fish, came over and peered into his engine and poked and prodded at all the various wires in there and after a while they all agreed that what Uncle Jack needed was a new Bendix which was news to him because he did not even know he had a Bendix in the first place.

The only Bendix he ever heard of besides William Bendix, the actor, was the old Bendix washer Mrs. Uncle Jack used to have which had a rubber tub which would collapse at just the right time and squeeze all the water out of the clothes. It worked real well, too, until the time Uncle Jack forgot and left his Swiss Army knife in his pocket with the corkscrew in the open position.

Anyway a nice man with a rifle in the back window of his pickup truck finally came along and gave him a tow and got his Jeep started again and he did not even wait for Uncle Jack to thank him before he was gone. If you want to know the truth Uncle Jack has never been too crazy about people who ride around with guns in their pickup trucks but he decided right then and there to send a generous contribution to the National Rifle Association and he is even thinking about voting for Charlton Heston if he ever runs for president.

It was a few minutes later before his radiator hose broke and that is another sad story but Uncle Jack does not wish to dwell any longer on his misfortunes. He can tell you he crossed the Bonner Bridge at sunset and what he saw was enough to make him forget all the trials and tribulations of the day.

And the ribs were not bad either.

Knowing How and Where to Fish

Uncle Jack is happy to report that this was another very good week for him in the fishing department. He followed Uncle Jack's First Law of Good Fishing which is to go where the fish are before you start fishing and it really paid off.

Last Saturday, for example, he was driving his new secondhand Jeep down on the beach on the way to work and he almost ran over this man who was busy catching a very large bluefish. Uncle Jack stopped right there and started trying to untangle his rusty Hopkins from the rest of the mess in his tackle box but then he saw a bottom rig which already had some mullet on the hooks from when he was fishing a few days before so he decided to try that. He does not expect anybody to believe it but two seconds after he casted out that bottom rig with the dried mullet on it he hooked a 17-pound bluefish which is the biggest fish he has caught in his life so far. If you ask him this ought to prove once and for all that as far as fishing goes if you are in the right place at the right time nothing else matters.

Uncle Jack has heard that this is also true in other walks of life such as real estate and bank robbery but he cannot vouch for that. But he does know about fishing so when he heard they were catching flounders down at

Cape Point last Sunday he drove right down there.

Uncle Jack and his friend who is a Professor of Philosophy over at N.C. State University caught so many flounders that they got tired out and had to stop fishing even before the flounders stopped biting. You might think that a Professor of Philosophy could not do anything practical like catch flounders but he really did which just goes to prove that if a person is in the right place at the right time he can overcome almost any handicap.

In between catching flounders Uncle Jack also caught his first octopus which he threw back because he does not have any good recipes for octopus. He is kicking himself, though, because somebody told him he probably had the new world record for octopus caught on 8-pound test line and he would have got his picture in the paper which he could have sent to all his relatives who thought he would never amount to anything.

Uncle Jack also caught a bluefish which clamped his teeth down hard on his finger and would not let go no matter how much he swore and jumped up and down. Finally Uncle Jack remembers this spy movie he saw on TV where these bad men were trying to get another man to talk so they held his head under water until he talked so Uncle Jack did the same thing to the bluefish and it really worked, too.

He held that bluefish's head under the water until he finally let go of Uncle Jack's finger and swam away which goes to prove that Uncle Jack is a lot smarter than your average bluefish. (OBX)

Uncle Jack
Braves the Storm

Uncle Jack is not by nature a gloomy person. His outlook on life is basically cheerful even though he realizes full well that he could be run over by a fish truck at any time.

"Every cloud has a silver lining," Uncle Jack insists. "It is always darkest before the dawn." Platitudes like these are the basic building blocks from which his serenity is formed.

This moderately optimistic *Weltanschauung* (Uncle Jack uses words like that whenever he can so that the pain of his high school education will not have been endured in vain) has made it possible for him to live contentedly on the Outer Banks.

A pessimist, Uncle Jack believes, could not possibly live on the Outer Banks because there is too much to worry about.

Take the melting polar ice caps, for example, which Uncle Jack did not learn about until the day after he sold his house in Pittsburgh three years ago.

"Are you sure you know what you are doing?" a friend asked him. "Surely you know that the polar ice caps are melting?"

Uncle Jack could not simply dismiss this peculiar warning as the ravings of a lunatic because it came from a Nobel Prize-winning scientist he used to play bridge with (which should give you some idea of the kind of circles Uncle Jack traveled in before he escaped to Nags Head).

What his friend was trying to tell him was that the polar ice caps are melting and making the ocean rise and in a couple hundred years, give or take a hundred or so, the Outer Banks will be under water. Needless to tell you, this friend has a low opinion of real estate here as a long-term investment.

If you want to know the truth Uncle Jack does not spend a lot of time worrying about the melting polar ice caps, but he has to confess that this is the time of the year when he does think a little about hurricanes once in a while.

Uncle Jack has had just enough experience with hurricanes to make him wonder what he should do when the next one comes along, as it surely will.

People who have lived around here for 50 years or more know a lot more about the kind of pickle we are going to be in when a big one happens again. All Uncle Jack has to go on was the little one he prayed through (imagine what it must have taken to get Uncle Jack down on his knees) one night back in September 1970.

Hurricane Ginger was a feeble little blow as hurricanes go, with maximum winds that never quite reached 100 miles an hour, but Uncle Jack will never forget that night as long as he lives.

For one thing it was the only time he ever saw rain come right through the walls (not the windows— the walls) of his house. Even so he was better off than his friends whose sliding glass doors blew out at 3 a.m. and let the wind and rain redecorate their apartment for two hours.

What worries Uncle Jack is that there are three (or maybe ten) times as many people on the Outer Banks in the hurricane season now then there were in 1970 and most of them do not have the foggiest notion of what a hurricane is like. And there are still only two bridges.

He can only hope that if a storm does come our way this year that every visitor and every resident will take it seriously. Come to think of it, Uncle Jack has never heard a hurricane joke and maybe that is a good sign.

Also he remembers that wonderful old saying, "It's an ill wind that blows nobody good."

Like if you happen to own a bulldozer for example.

OBX

DON'T TOUCH ANYTHING
A One-Act Play
Written for
the Theatre of the Absurd

CHARACTERS:
Clerk
Male parent
Female parent
Three young children.

SCENE: A souvenir shop somewhere on the Outer Banks of North
Carolina. It is 11 a.m. on a typically
hot and humid August day.

SETTING: Clerk hastily gulps her
fourth Valium of the morning as
three tow-headed children, ages
5, 4 and 2 burst through the door,
followed moments later by their
tanned but haggard-looking parents, mother carrying a small baby.

CLERK:
(feigning cheerfulness born of economic necessity):
"Morning, folks. Can I help you?"

MALE PARENT:
"No, thanks. Just browsing."

FEMALE PARENT:
"I don't want you kids to touch
NOTHING, understand?"

Her eyes glazed, FEMALE PARENT
apparently is unable to perceive
that her three ambulatory children are simultaneously touching
47 breakable objects even as she
speaks.

FIVE-YEAR-OLD brandishes a
ceramic replica of Cape Hatteras
Lighthouse, exquisitely crafted by
skilled Korean artisans and au-
thentic in every respect except for
the mauve and yellow stripes.

FIVE-YEAR-OLD:
"Mommy I want one of these get
me one I want one PLEASE."

FEMALE PARENT:
"Rocky, I told you not to touch anything. Now put that back where you got it right now and DON'T TOUCH ANYTHING!!"

FIVE-YEAR-OLD:
"I hate you. You never buy me nothing I want."

Five-year-old aims vicious kick at table containing 200 plastic replicas of Wright brothers' first glider.

FOUR-YEAR-OLD:
"Daddy, I has to go tee tee."

Male Parent is deeply engrossed in a study of poster displaying esthetically pleasing array of deeply bronzed and oiled female torsos.

MALE PARENT:
"Huh?"

FOUR-YEAR-OLD:
"Daddy, I has to go tee tee real bad."

MALE PARENT
(to Female Parent, who is un-
successfully attempting to quiet
screaming infant):
"Debbie has to go, Hon. Can you
take her somewhere?"

FEMALE PARENT
(shouting to clerk over screams of
deranged infant):
"You got a bathroom in here?"

CLERK
(praying that the Lord will not
strike her dead for telling a mon-
strous lie):
"I'm sorry but the nearest bathroom is over at the Visitor's Center
in Kitty Hawk which is about 12
miles from here so you better get
going before it's too late."

TWO-AND-A-HALF-YEAR-OLD
knocks over pyramid display con-
structed of 750 imported ceramic
ashtrays inscribed "Fun in the
Sun—Nags Heap, N.C.," which had
taken the owner three slow days in
June to stack.

TWO-AND-A-HALF-YEAR-OLD:
"Waaaaaaah!"

FEMALE PARENT:
"Dammit, Rambo, I told you not to touch nothin'. Now put those things back where they were because we got to go."

MALE PARENT
(still ogling oiled nudes):
"Why don't you take the kids out to the car, Hon, while I buy this poster for the family room."

CLERK
(reaching for Valium bottle as first family departs and new group enters):
"Y'all come back soon, hear?"

CURTAIN

Olympic Porchsitting

Lucky for Uncle Jack the Olympic Committee has not made Porchsitting into one of the official games yet because he is not too crazy about the idea of being in Atlanta at this time of the year, especially if he had to engage in serious competition with the best Porchsitters from all over the world in all that heat and humidity they have down there.

He knows it is only a matter of time before Porchsitting gets approved as an official Olympic Game because the AARP has been lobbying pretty hard for it the past couple of years and they usually get what they want.

Anyway he is going to keep honing his Porchsitting skills which he feels are already world-class in some areas such as Osprey Appreciation, Porpoise-Spotting, Gull-Feed from the Prone Position, Pelican-Counting and Synchronized Rocking (with Mrs. Uncle Jack). He needs more polishing in a few others like Avoiding Eye Contact With the Renters Next Door. He still has a tendency to let himself be drawn into banal conversations which cause him to lose concentration and which could cost him points in international competition.

But enough pontificating. It is time for Uncle Jack to return to the porch for another grueling practice session. When the time comes to porchsit for his country he will be ready.

He could also use a nice chair contract.

Hatteras Lite

Dear Uncle Jack,

I have to tell you I am really tired of hearing about the Hatteras lighthouse. What is such a big deal about lighthouses, anyway? Nobody needs them anymore since they invented radar and sonar and all that stuff so why spend a lot of money trying to keep a lighthouse from falling down when there are so many other things that we really need like an elevated highway from Oregon Inlet to Buxton?

You're pretty smart,

Uncle Jack, so I presume you are in agreement with me that they ought to let the lighthouse fall in the drink, but I wouldn't be surprised if you were too chicken to come right out and admit it in public.

Len Fresnel
Avon

Dear Len,

First of all, Uncle Jack would like to say that if he thought it would be best to let the lighthouse fall in the ocean he would come right out and say it. He is not running for office so there is no reason for him to lie about what he really thinks.

Right now he is leaning toward letting it fall in the ocean, primarily because it would be so much fun to watch on TV. Uncle Jack has seen those movies on TV where they put a lot of dynamite in a building and blow it up and the whole thing falls down in a big heap of rubble and he never fails to get a big kick out of watching that, especially when they do it in slow motion about six times. He can hardly imagine what a thrill it would be to watch that lighthouse fall into the ocean due to natural causes without the use of any artificial devices such as dynamite.

Uncle Jack is pretty sure that an event like this would get terrific ratings on TV and if the people in charge of the lighthouse played their cards right they could make enough money out of it to build a much nicer, higher lighthouse with all the amenities such as jacuzzis and elevators and skyboxes where the big corporations could entertain politicians and other important people and write it off as a business expense.

If Uncle Jack was in charge he would start right away to put out a line of T-shirts, each one of which would have a day, hour and minute printed on it, and the proceeds would go into a pool and the person who has the closest time to when the lighthouse falls down would win a nice prize like breakfast at Sam and Omie's and the rest of the money would go toward building a bigger and better lighthouse in a safer place like over behind the reverse osmosis plant.

The present lighthouse is not the first one at Hatteras or even the second so it is not as though something like this has never happened before. Each succeeding lighthouse has been bigger and better than the one before and there is no reason this could not be the case again. Everybody would have to watch out to make sure the contractors did not try to build it out of particle board but that does not seem like an insurmountable problem.

Uncle Jack has many more ideas about how to deal with the lighthouse quandary but he is running out of space and will have to save them for the future, assuming there is one.*

Optimistically,
Uncle Jack

---

* NOTE: Undoubtedly to Uncle Jack's chagrin, the Hatteras Lighthouse later would be moved to safety. There is always next time, however.

(OBX)

Uncle Jack Knows

Of Sailboats and Sunsets and Fits of Thinking

As Uncle Jack grows older he is seized more and more by uncontrollable fits of philosophizing. He never knows when these attacks will come, and he is helpless to control them. Fortunately these spells of pontificating usually pass before he has time to bore more than a few close friends and relatives.

Uncle Jack has been afflicted most recently by deep thoughts about the nature of time. He has reached an age that enables him to confirm the widely held belief that time seems to speed up as one grows older. He had often heard this said by older persons, but older persons have told him so many things that turned out not to be true that he has never been sure he could believe anything they say.

But now he knows from his own experience that time does indeed pass more rapidly as one grows older. It took approximately 25 years for Uncle Jack to get from age 12 to 18 but it took only about two weeks to get from his 40th birthday to his 50th.

At this rate he expects to turn 75 sometime around the middle of next week.

This remarkable speeding up of time can be scary enough to set off some fairly weird behavior in folks who are in Uncle Jack's age bracket. Men and women who have been dutifully traveling down life's highway for half a century or so sometimes accidentally look up just long enough to see a tractor trailer with a skull and crossbones on it bearing down on them. Metaphorically speaking, of course.

Some folks go trudging on and don't even try to get out of the way. Others make some remarkable moves in an effort to dodge that truck. Uncle Jack met two such agile people last week on the waterfront in Manteo.

The couple, on the early side of middle age, took their big leap about a year ago—divesting themselves of cars, televisions, lawnmowers and mortgages—all the encumbrances of solid middle-class existence. They used the proceeds from their years of straight-arrow effort to build themselves the pretty little sailboat that you may have seen at the Manteo dock last week.

They live on their boat now, going wherever they please whenever they please. Soon or later when their money runs out, they'll be back in the middle of the road with the rest of us—but what memories they'll have on those nights when there's nothing to watch on television.

Uncle Jack must say, however, that he felt not even the slightest twinge of envy when the intrepid couple sailed off to New York City last week. Why anyone would voluntarily go to New York when he could stay in Manteo is beyond his feeble powers of comprehension.

The other event of last week that seemed to set off this fit of deep thinking was the sunset of Thursday evening, July 30. Uncle Jack will wisely refrain from attempting to describe that sunset; it was truly ineffable (a word he memorized in high school, knowing that it would come in handy some day).

Suffice it to say that the sunset was so magnificent that it started Uncle Jack philosophizing so hard he thought he was going to have a stroke.

The message in all this, he thinks, is that as we trudge down life's highway we should not be afraid to look up once in a while. We might see a big truck bearing down on us, but on the other hand we might see a sunset that will knock his socks off.

Whew.

Whatever this is, Uncle Jack hopes he will be over it by next week.

Of Pipe Dreams
and
Theological Inquiries

You might not believe it when Uncle Jack tells you winter is his very favorite time of year on the Outer Banks.

Being a high school graduate he is naturally the kind of person who does a lot of hard thinking, and if you need a lot of time to think there is no better place to be than the Outer Banks in winter.

If you want to know the truth Uncle Jack will do more heavy thinking during the next two months than he will do in all the rest of the year put together.

He will have plenty of time to sit down, or even lie down for that matter, and really grapple with some of those great questions of human existence that have puzzled philsophers and other smart persons for several years.

By which Uncle Jack means such vital questions as, What is Truth? What is Justice? What is Beauty? And What's the Use?

"What's the Use?" is actually the question Uncle Jack has been asking himself most often since Christmas Eve when his pipes froze up again for the 38th time in the last three years.

What's the use of trying to be honest and moral and upright and kind to animals, he asks himself, if his pipes are going to freeze up anyway?

If Uncle Jack had known this is the way it was going to be he would have said to hell with it and gone to law school a long time ago.

Also Uncle Jack cannot help wondering what God had in mind when He froze all those pipes on Christmas Eve and made so many people miserable when they should have been happy.

Was he trying to tell us sinners something, Uncle Jack wonders, or was it just an honest mistake? Uncle Jack would like to believe that He really meant to freeze a lot of pipes over in Russia but his computer broke down or something.

Also Uncle Jack cannot help wondering about all those people whose pipes did not freeze up on Christmas Eve. Was God sending them a sign that they are more worthy than the rest of us?

Anyway, you might be getting the idea that Uncle Jack is going to spend the rest of the winter pondering the theology of frozen pipes but that is not what he plans to do.

There are too many other important questions he must find time to grapple with before the tourists get here and start shoving money in his hands again, to wit:

- How did the crickets get into the ceiling fixture in Uncle Jack's kitchen? And why?

- Will Uncle Jack's new secondhand Jeep oxidize completely and disappear before he makes the final bank payment on September 13?

- Will the new Food Lion make Uncle Jack forget all about the Safeway by using beer as a loss leader?

- What should Uncle Jack do if his bottled gas company takes another four-day vacation during the next bad cold spell?

- How will Super Cable affect the future course of Uncle Jack's intellectual development? Will he suffer further brain damage?

And finally, that perennial question, for which he will continue to seek an answer until he is carried to his final resting place in the paupers' cemetery: Why does gasoline cost 20 cents a gallon more on the Outer Banks than it does in Greenville?

Have a real nice winter, hear?

Come
on Down

Dear Uncle Jack,

I am one of those unfortunate people who gets to spend his two week summer vacation on the Outer Banks and then he is miserable the rest of the year because he is not down there.

Believe me I would have quit my lousy job at Cleveland Gear and Screw and moved down there years ago except for my wife who does not think she could stand it down there in the winter with nothing to do to keep her brain alive.

We have been married for 42 years and raised 13 children so I do not feel it would be right just to dump her, especially since I got laid off at Cleveland Gear and Screw right before Christmas and my unemployment is due to run out this month.

You probably read in the paper where Cleveland Gear got out of the machine parts business and into frozen pierogies and they are doing real good, too, but I could never get the hang of that computerized potato peeler they put me on so they canned me without so much as a Timex after 35 years.

So now I mostly shovel snow out of the driveway and count the days until my wife gets her annual vacation from the Burger Bistro over on Cuyahoga Avenue. They made her the manager over there after only two days on the job when they found out she could read and write, both.

Anyway, I know things are changing fast on the Outer Banks and winter isn't like it used to be down there so I was hoping you could say a few words of encouragement to my wife so she would at least start thinking about the possibility of maybe moving down there for good some day.

Milo Minderbinder
Cleveland, OH

Dear Milo,

Uncle Jack receives many letters from unhappy persons such as yourself and he is pleased to tell you he has good news for all of you.

You are absolutely right when you say that winter is not like it used to be in the old days when winter started the day after Labor Day and ended on Memorial Day. If you want to know the truth, it has got to the point where you can hardly tell the difference between winter down here and winter in Cleveland except we do not have any snow down here which is not bad at all if you ask Uncle Jack.

As far as new cultural development, Uncle Jack hardly knows where to start. For one thing they are building a big addition onto the bowling alley and they are planning to bring the Pro Bowlers tour in here next winter which the wife will have to admit is a major cultural event and a big step up from those tacky karate fights they put on over at Roller World last year.

In case the Mrs. is into more intellectual pursuits Uncle Jack should mention the Great Books discussion

club they have over at the Old Folks Center in Kill Devil
Hills every Thursday night.

They started out with *Lady Chatterly's Lover* last
month and they are working their way up to Sidney Shel-
don's best-selling trilogy *Lust*, *Depravity*, and *More Lust
and Depravity* and Uncle Jack can tell you those discussions have already got to the point where they have to
station a whole EMS crew over there every Thursday night
just to watch out for heart attacks.

Also Uncle Jack would be remiss if he did not
mention that you can get 28 different channels on the TV
cable down here now not counting HBO and Cinemax so
there really is not any good reason to go out of the house
between Thanksgiving and Memorial Day unless you run
out of food and beverages (which the Home Shopping
Club has not gotten into yet).

Anyway, it is a whole new ball game down here in
the winter and there is no reason why your wife should not
be happy.

So like they always say on *The Price is Right*,
"Come on Down!!"

> Cheerfully,
> Uncle Jack

Shredded Hopes

Dear Uncle Jack,

I spent two weeks on the Outer Banks last summer and now I spend most of my time trying to figure out

how I could make a living down there. I have a terrific job running a shredding machine for the C.I.A. and I'm really good at it so I was wondering if you knew anybody down there who is looking for an experienced shredder. I could be there tomorrow if they need me and if the hours were right I would even consider working for less than the $275,000 I'm making now. I won't sleep until I hear from you, Uncle Jack, so please hurry.

                                     Anxious
                                     McLean, Virginia

Dear Anxious,

Uncle Jack is certainly glad to hear that you would be willing to take a modest pay cut because that will help you a lot when you go looking for a job down here. He is not sure what they are paying paper shredders over at the county office building but he doubts if it's anywhere near $275,000. They have surprised him before, though, so you might want to check it out when you get down here.

The big problem you face, though, is that there just aren't that many openings for paper shredders down here due to the general lack of large scale covert activity. There is probably a little hanky panky from time to time in some of the lawyers' offices but most of it usually gets torn up by hand and flushed down the toilet.

What it boils down to if you ask Uncle Jack, and you did, is that you might have to go into some other line of work, or at least you might have to adapt your highly developed shredding skills to something other than paper.

Have you thought about cabbage? There is hardly a restaurant on the Outer Banks that doesn't have to make a ton of coleslaw every day and that means shredding a lot of cabbage. You might think about picking up a government surplus high performance shredder and setting yourself up in the wholesale coleslaw business.

If you want to know the truth that is about the only business he can think of that there is not at least two of already on the Outer Banks. For example if you are thinking about opening a discount department store forget it. There is already a Walmart and a Kmart down here and that's at least one too many if you ask Uncle Jack.

He knows how you feel about wanting to move to the Outer Banks, though, because he had the same problem once, a long time ago. All he can say is that if you want to live here badly enough you will find a way.

Optimistically,
Uncle Jack

P.S. How do you feel about selling real estate?

Don't Make a Move

Dear Uncle Jack,

I am one of the two million Pennsylvania residents who are planning to move to the Outer Banks to live as soon as they can figure out some way to swing it. You have been living there for quite a while now, Uncle Jack, and I was wondering if you had any advice for us.

Envious Eddy
Johnstown, Pa.

Dear Eddy,

You are right about one thing. Uncle Jack is getting to be quite an old-timer on the Outer Banks.

Just last week he was looking at his Acme Auto Parts calendar. All of a sudden it dawned on him that it is 1984 and he has been living down here for four years now and the way things are changing on the Outer Banks these days four years is a pretty long time.

Uncle Jack really enjoys being an old-timer, too, because he can rear back in his rocking chair and tell all kinds of stories about what it was like in the old days when men were men—back before the Seamark when you had to drive all the way to Norfolk every time you wanted cilantro in your salad.

He can remember some really amazing things like the day they brought in the first prefabricated condominium on a truck for example. If you want to know the truth Uncle Jack and the first prefabricated condominium arrived on the Outer Banks at about the same time and he is not quite sure what to make of that. It could be an omen of some kind but he is not sure.

Anyway he could go on and on about all the amazing things that have happened around here in the past four years but if he did he would not have room to give you the advice you asked for which is DON'T MOVE DOWN HERE! Stay in Johnstown and pray for another flood and you will be better off.

You sound like one of those people who came down here and spent a few days on vacation and caught some fish and had a good time and now you think you want to live here. Well Uncle Jack has lived here long enough to tell you that life on the Outer Banks is not just one long vacation. You have to be able to put up with a lot of hardship and frustration like Uncle Jack did last Sunday which he is going to tell you about so brace yourself.

Last Sunday Uncle Jack drove all the way down to Cape Hatteras in his new secondhand Jeep which is now 24 pounds lighter than it was when he bought it which he knows because that is how much rust he has swept up out of the driveway since last September.

Anyway he drove for hours through that government refuge down there where all you ever see is weird looking birds and juvenile delinquents trying to dig their vans out of the sand and finally he got to Cape Point and started fishing. He fished his heart out for two hours and he used up an entire $1.50 mullet for bait and HE NEVER GOT A BITE!

And neither did Mrs. Uncle Jack or their friends so they had to give up and just sat there in the sun and drank beer and ate fried chicken instead of catching fish which is what they drove all the way down there to do in the first place.

After a while they drove up to Ramp 23 by Salvo and they fished for a long time and they used up another whole mullet and THEY NEVER GOT A BITE! By then the beer was gone and the fried chicken was gone so all they could do was go home and make a pitcher of martinis and sit on the deck and watch the sun go down over Roanoke Sound and talk about what a rotten day it had been.

Anyway that should give you an idea of the kind of disappointment and frustration and heartache you would have to live with all the time if you moved down here. If you have plenty of beer and fried chicken up there in Johnstown take Uncle Jack's advice and stay there. You will be a lot happier in the long run.

Sagely,
Uncle Jack

Labor Day
by
George

There was a time not so many years ago that Labor Day had some real significance on the Outer Banks because it meant the end of another summer season. The pace of life suddenly slowed and local merchants, store-bound since Memorial Day, would emerge, blinking, into the sunlight, seeking the healing balm of the ocean like newly hatched sea turtles. (Uncle Jack can really wax lyrical when it comes to Labor Day.)

After Labor Day the tourists pretty much vanished, taking with them their wallets and credit cards, so there was little incentive to keep stores and restaurants open any longer. The late George Crocker, who more than 40 years ago brought modern concepts of merchandising to the Outer Banks with his futuristic Galleon Esplanade, officially signaled the end of the season with his gala "Gambler's Sale," for many years the premier social event of the year for tourists and locals alike.

George would don one of his most flamboyant ensembles and spend the day spinning a huge roulette wheel marked off in segments reading "20% off" up to "50% off" (and even one narrow sliver marked "FREE"). Eager customers would queue to wait for their chance to thrust a slightly shop-worn dress or bathing suit or an imported ceramic likeness of a seashell into George's hands and watch him spin the wheel that could bring them unheard of savings on the merchandise of their dreams. Only the most cynical observers (Uncle Jack among them) would note that even at 50% off the stuff was overpriced, but who could care when the cheers of hordes of onlookers greeted every spin of the wheel?

Those glorious days are gone forever (along with George and the Galleon) and the arrival of Labor Day on the Outer Banks is about as significant as the advent of Christmas in the bazaars of Abu Dhabi. Half the work force has fled the area to return to schools that opened (against the laws of nature if you ask Uncle Jack) in mid-August forcing exhausted merchants to work even longer hours than before. In a very real sense Labor Day has come to mean "from now on you are really going to have to labor," especially now that more and more entrepreneurs are chasing fewer and fewer dollars.

For the first ten years after he discovered the Outer Banks, Labor Day had an even greater poignancy for Uncle Jack. It meant that it was time to close up the cottage, pack up the car and return to the real world of Pittsburgh where he would be forced to live in a kind of smoky limbo for nine months, struggling to breathe and pining all the while for his beloved Nags Head.

He hasn't had to do that for over 20 years now and that is the reason why, with all the violence that has been done to the concept of Labor Day (and to the Outer Banks in general) since he moved here, he still considers himself a very lucky old dude.

As far as he is concerned there is no better place in the world to be overworked, and judging from the proliferation of businesses around here, there must be a lot of people who agree with him. Hang in there, merchants. With 116 shopping days left (if you stay open seven days a week) you still have a chance to break even before Christmas.

Winter Fun

Dear Uncle Jack,

I see by the calendar that winter is half over and I was wondering how you are holding up down there on the bleak, windswept, Godforsaken Outer Banks. I have always admired the raw courage and endurance of the brave men and women such as yourself who somehow manage to survive

down there winter after winter with nothing to do but listen to the wind howl and watch houses topple into the sea.

The wife and I have been reading about all the terrible storms you have had down there already this winter and we want you to know that we are praying for you and also our timeshare in Duck.

Fairweather Friend,
Seawall, N.J.

Dear Friend,

Relax. Uncle Jack is happy to tell you that winter on the Outer Banks is not half as bad as you would think from reading the papers. For one thing blowing sand is not much of a problem anymore because most of the sand is covered with asphalt. Uncle Jack can tell you it takes a pretty good wind to blow the sand out from under a parking lot to the point where it makes any real trouble.

You still have to be on your toes when the wind blows hard, though, especially when you are downwind of some of those prefab condos which are not always stapled together quite as well as they could be. Uncle Jack has never personally been hit by a flying jacuzzi but he imagines it would be a lot like being blindsided by Lawrence Taylor.

As far as Uncle Jack knows there is only one place left on the Outer Banks where blowing sand is still a big problem and that is over at Jockey's Ridge in Nags Head. They should have let nature take its course over there and just let it get paved over like everything else but instead some do-gooders made it into a state park a few years ago and now it is the biggest single source of sand pollution on the whole Outer Banks.

Anyway, Uncle Jack is pleased to tell you there is a lot more to do down here these days than just listen to the wind blow. For one thing he can sit in the comfort of his living room and watch a dozen giant earth movers chase the bunnies out of the golf course they are building by his house and he can tell you he does not want to be around there next spring when the copperhead snakes come out of their holes and find out what has been going on in their neighborhood.

Sometimes after Uncle Jack has finished watching the bulldozers he goes out to dinner at one of the many fine restaurants which are now open all winter and he can tell you they are all doing their best to keep up with the latest culinary trends, too. As far as Uncle Jack is concerned if you have not tasted blackened bluefish with a side of collards Nicoise you are just not living life to the fullest.

After dinner Uncle Jack sits in his chair and listens to the sirens up on the Bypass and he can close his eyes and imagine that he is in New York City and he can hardly remember what it was like around here in the old days— five years ago.

Contentedly,
Uncle Jack

Safe
at Home

Uncle Jack read in the paper last week where the Amtrak train company is having a big sale on tickets. They are selling tickets so cheap that even if you are somebody like Uncle Jack who never wants to leave the Outer Banks it makes you wonder if there isn't some place you should go visit even though you don't want to.

For instance you can ride the train to California and back for $200 which is less than you would have to pay to sit in a motel room in Mann's Harbor for the same length of time. Also they will let you get off the train twice to go sightseeing and they do not charge you anything to get back on.

Right away when he read that, Uncle Jack started trying to think of two places he would like to see in California but the only one he could think of was Disneyland. Somebody told him they have a mechanical statue of President Abraham Lincoln out there that stands up and recites the whole Gettysburg Address by heart and then sits down again. That is something

Uncle Jack has never been able to do himself so he would really like to see a statue do it.

He was starting to talk himself into going out there on the train but then he read in the paper where a crazy person with a rifle was shooting at Disneyland from his motel room so Uncle Jack decided he would just take their word about that statue of Abraham Lincoln.

Before he could think of any other place in California he would like to visit, Uncle Jack read in the paper where this Amtrak train ran off the tracks in Texas and a lot of people got killed and injured. That was the end of that. Now they could give him tickets free and they still could not get Uncle Jack to take the train to California. If he is going to have to worry about getting killed all the way out there and all the way back, he would rather do it on an airplane where he would only have to hold his breath for a few hours.

If you want to know the truth he did not want to go to California anyway and why should he when there are so many interesting things to do right here on the Outer Banks? For example he could spend the whole month of November just standing on the beach and watching the seagulls swooping and diving over those schools of big bluefish that always seem to be about 10 yards farther out than Uncle Jack can cast.

And when he gets tired of doing that, he can turn around and watch the seagulls stealing the fresh mullet out of the back of his new secondhand Jeep. Either way there is never a dull moment on the beach in November.

There was never a dull moment at the Manteo High School football game last night either. That was the first high school football game Uncle Jack has gone to since he was in high school himself back during the dark ages before TV and it sure did send him into a fit of nostalgia there for a while.

For one thing, he had almost forgotten how much fun it is to sit on a cold iron bench for several hours with the wind blowing out of the north at 20 miles an hour. Also he had almost forgotten all those so-called grown-ups who go to high school football games and spend the whole time talking about how dumb the coach is and cursing the players who make mistakes and screaming "Kill him!!!" every time the other team's quarterback gets tackled. Uncle Jack wishes people like that would just stay home and watch *Rambo* movies on TV.

Also when he saw all the high school boys trying to impress their cute dates and all their cute dates trying not to be impressed he was very glad he does not have to go through high school again because he does not think he could make it.

Anyway, Uncle Jack is glad he went to the football game because now he is pretty sure he can get through another 35 years without seeing another one. Also he is glad he could finally forget about going to California and get back to the simple pleasures of off-season life on the Outer Banks such as eating dead oysters and not waiting in line at the grocery store.

SUDDENLY LAST SUMMER
A One-Act Play
By Pier Andello
Written for the Theatre of the Absurd

CHARACTERS:
Uncle Jack, the kindly old proprietor
Male tourist
Female tourist
Male tourist No. 2
Female tourist No. 2

SETTING: A small poster gallery and framing shop somewhere on the Outer Banks.

SCENE ONE

TIME: Mid-morning on an overcast Wednesday in early June, only a few days into a new tourist season.

UNCLE JACK:
Mornin' folks. Can I help ...

MALE TOURIST
and FEMALE TOURIST
(in unison):

Just browsing.

UNCLE JACK:
Where you folks from?

MALE TOURIST:

Ahia

UNCLE JACK:
Wow! What part of Ahia?

MALE TOURIST:

Up by Canton.

UNCLE JACK:
Ah, yes. Canton. Home of the
Bulldogs.

MALE TOURIST:

Huh?

UNCLE JACK:
Bulldogs. Used to be a famous
football team.

MALE TOURIST:
Musta been before my time.

UNCLE JACK:
I used to live in Pittsburgh,
which is right up by Ohio.

MALE TOURIST:
No kidding. I used to have a
cousin lived in Pittsburgh.

UNCLE JACK:
It's a small world, that's for
sure. Your first visit to the Outer
Banks?

MALE TOURIST:
Nope. Been comin' down here
for 25 years.

UNCLE JACK:
Wow. You must like it down
here.

MALE TOURIST:
Used to like it a lot more. Too
many people down here now.
They're wreckin' the place.

UNCLE JACK:
Who's wreckin' the place?

MALE TOURIST:
All them developers. They ought
to string 'em up.

Uncle Jack drives a No. 3 finishing nail into
his left index finger.

UNCLE JACK:

Damn!

FEMALE TOURIST:
There ought to be a law against
all this building.

UNCLE JACK
(sagely):
It's a free country, you know.
You can't stop people from
building on their own property.

MALE TOURIST:
Well, you better do something
before it's too late. Nobody from
Ahia is gonna wanna come
down here anymore if you keep
this up.

UNCLE JACK
(sagely):
Well, it's not half as bad as a
lot of other places and besides,
all these new stores and everything mean jobs for a lot of
people. I'll bet if all this growth
was happening up in Canton
a lot of people would be happy
about it.

MALE TOURIST looks away in disgust as
Uncle Jack neatly slices off tip of left index
finger with mat knife.

MALE TOURIST:
I don't care. We came down here
to get away from all the noise
and traffic and people, and now
it's all down here, too.

UNCLE JACK
(sagely):
Well, you might as well try to
get used to it and enjoy yourselves because there is nothing you or anybody else can do
about it and it's going to keep on
like this right up to the next bad

hurricane and then will start all
over again.

MALE TOURIST:
Well, Myrt. See anything you
like?

FEMALE TOURIST:
(brandishing swatch of
maroon naugahyde):
Can't find anything that goes
with the couch. You got any
other art galleries around here
might have a seascape with maroon in it?

UNCLE JACK:
You could try Walmart.

MALE TOURIST:
Nice talking to you, son. You
take care of that finger, and look
us up if you ever get to Canton.

UNCLE JACK:
Y'all come back now, hear?

SCENE TWO

Time: Ten minutes later.

UNCLE JACK:
Morning, folks. Can I help ...

MALE TOURIST 2
and FEMALE TOURIST 2
(in unison):
Just browsing.

UNCLE JACK:
Where you folks from?

MALE TOURIST 2:

Ahia.

UNCLE JACK:
(dropping crate of
glass on foot):

Damn!

CURTAIN

(OBX)

Wright Thinking

Aside from the coming nuclear holocaust there isn't a whole lot that Uncle Jack worries about very much. Living here on the Outer Banks he is surrounded by so much beauty all the time that it's hard for him to concentrate on troublesome things.

There is one thing that bothers Uncle Jack just a little bit, though, and it happens every December just when the eyes of the whole world are focused on the Outer Banks as we celebrate yet another anniversary of the Wright brothers' first successful flight.

Unfortunately, it is this same week that a noisy, besotted band of malcontents who call themselves the "Man Will Never Fly Society" come here for their annual convention. These crazy people run around trying to convince people that airplanes are nothing more than hallucinations and that the Wright brothers actually invented the bus, not the airplane.

These people are going to give the Outer Banks a bad name if they keep it up. People who don't live here are bound to think that this is what happens

when you try to live all year round on some godforsaken barrier island where the wind blows your brains
loose. You get to drinking and playing poker and the
next thing you know you're saying weird things like
"man will never fly" and actually believing them.

Uncle Jack has never heard them offer any
proof that airplanes can't fly. All you have to do, they
say, is look at a 747 and you know there's no way it's
going to get off the ground except maybe with a der-
rick.

Well Uncle Jack has got news for them. He has
been watching the geese and swans out in the sound
in back of his house for the past couple of weeks and
says if those silly creatures with their big fat bodies
and their itty bitty wings can fly, so can airplanes.

Also, Uncle Jack has noticed, these people are
male chauvinist pigs. "Birds fly, men drink," is their
motto and where, Uncle Jack wonders, does that leave
the women? How are they supposed to get through
the winter while the geese and swans are flying all over
the place and the men are too drunk to get up from the
poker table?

Uncle Jack's advice to this weird bunch of
rumpots who call themselves the "Man Will Never Fly
Society" is to cool it. You embarrass the rest of us
Wright-thinking Outer Bankers just when we should
all be contemplating the wonderful advances in human
culture the airplane has brought us, like overnight de-
livery of Chivas Regal from Scotland, and saturation
bombing.

Joy of Retail

Dear Uncle Jack,

Last week you wrote about how awful it is to run a retail store and have to put up with kids running around and wrecking stuff and babies crying and all that. Well if you ask me, that is only one side of the story because I have been behind the counter for almost 45 years and I can honestly tell you I have enjoyed nearly every minute of it, kids and all.

As far as I am concerned there is no other job in the world where you get to meet so many interesting people and there is never a dull moment. For example just last week this couple from Canton, Ohio, came into the store who have been married 52 years and they do not have any children or grandchildren and they do not have a Winnebago and they have never been to Disney World.

You do not meet fascinating people like this very often if you are in some dull field like accounting or brain surgery and that is why retail is so interesting and exciting for me. I hate to say this but it sounds to me like you are too grouchy to have a very rewarding career in retail and maybe you should go into some other line of work such as law enforcement where you can hit people with a club or shoot them if you don't like what they are doing.

Macy Bloomingdale
Manteo

Dear Macy,

Uncle Jack would like to thank you for taking valuable time away from your cash register to write and give him your views on a subject that is near and dear to your heart and also his.

He did not mean to give the impression that he does not enjoy his life in retail because nothing could be further from the truth. He cannot think of anybody in the world that he would want to trade places with except maybe Hugh Hefner and he hopes he can go right on retailing until the perfect end which would be where he would drop dead in ecstasy right after some customer bought $999 worth of pictures and paid for them with ten $100 bills.

Uncle Jack agrees with you that there is no job where you can meet so many interesting people every day as you can behind the counter of a retail store. And he is not talking about the kind of people you meet on the graveyard shift at the 7-Eleven either. He means the kind of people you can meet in any retail store on the Outer Banks at any time and he will give you an example.

During the slow period right after lunch one day last week Uncle Jack was busy scraping bubble gum off the carpet when in walks this nice-looking middle-aged woman wearing one of those leather helmets like you see on wimp hockey players sometimes. This was one of the hottest days of the year not to mention humid and he will tell you this woman was a sweaty mess top to bottom and if you want to know the truth she did not smell too good either.

It turns out she was riding her bicycle from Orlando, Florida, to Washington, D.C., and she and Uncle Jack had a nice chat about how much fun she would have the next day riding her bike up Route 158 through Currituck County which is two-lane most of the way with soft shoulders while he would be spending just another ordinary day cooped up in his little air-conditioned store.

He can tell you she really got him thinking about what he was missing in the adventure department and for a while there he was thinking maybe he should chuck the whole retail way of life and get himself a 10-speed and chase her up the road.

Then he looked at the thermometer and thought about it some more and he decided he would be better off if he stayed right in his store and waited for another interesting person to come in instead.

> Have a nice day,
> Uncle Jack

PETA

Dear Uncle Jack,

I read in the paper where some crazy people from up north are going around trying to get people to stop fishing. They say it is not fair for people to kill fish to eat and it is even worse for people to fish for "sport" which is where you get fish to bite on hooks and drag them through the water for a while and then let them go. They say the hooks hurt the fishes' mouths and is not fair for humans to hurt fish just because they are bigger.

Is that the dumbest thing you ever heard of or what, Uncle Jack?

Skip Charter
Hatteras Village

Dear Skip,

Uncle Jack would hesitate to say this is the dumbest thing he ever heard of because he used to attend a lot of commissioners' meetings back when he was a reporter and he heard some doozies there, too.

He does have to admit, though, that when he first heard about People for the Ethical Treatment of Animals which is what they call themselves he thought maybe they were all suffering from some kind of protein deprivation or something.

He does try to give people the benefit of the doubt even when they seem like worthy objects of ridicule so he has been pondering the whole business of the food chain and man's place in it a lot lately, especially during the late evening when he is likely to be consuming only distilled vegetable matter which is not likely to offend any pressure groups with the possible exception of the WCTU if there still is one. As far as he knows there is not yet a group called People for the Ethical Treatment of Barley for which many of us can be thankful.

Anyway Uncle Jack has been reading as much as he can find about what the PETA folks say about "ethical treatment of animals" and he has to admit they make some pretty good points and he is not going to read any more because if they talked him into treating animals fairly it could really mess up his life, especially at mealtimes.

It is very hard for Uncle Jack to contemplate a life

without hamburgers, hot dogs, pork chops, chicken wings, filet mignons, fish sandwiches and all the other non-vegetable stuff he eats every day. He tries not to think about where the hamburger came from or how the cow felt when she got whacked over the head with a sledgehammer or however they do it these days. (Maybe they get whacked over the head with computers.)

On the other hand Uncle Jack is not inclined to poke too much fun at people who are nice enough to try to understand how a cow or chicken or pig might feel about sacrificing his or her life to satisfy some person's craving for a Big Mac or a plate of spicy Buffalo Wings.

About fish Uncle Jack is not so sure. He does not know whether or not fish experience physical distress or even angst when pierced by a hook and dragged through the water against their presumed wills. He can tell you at one time he thought that matching wits with a wily fish (estimated brain weight 1/4 ounce) was man's noblest sport. Now he doesn't even own a rod and reel.

But how he loves those fish sandwiches at Sam and Omie's.

Ice Plant Island

Dear Uncle Jack,

I read in the paper where they are trying to think up a new name for Ice Plant Island, which would make it sound classier for the tourists. Some people want to call it New World Park and other people want to call it Roanoke

Festival Park* and other people want to name it after Wanchese or Manteo or some of the other natives who lived
around here in the old days before the first outlet mall.

   I know you probably thought about this a lot yourself, Uncle Jack, so I would like to know what you think
they should call it.

Common Mann
Mann's Harbor

Dear Common,

   The guiding principle of Uncle Jack's life so far has
been "do whatever is easiest" and this is the main reason
why he thinks they should just leave it Ice Plant Island.
Everybody who lives around here knows where Ice Plant
Island is so if they are in a good mood they can tell the
tourists how to get there.

   If they change the name to something fancy like
Roanoke Festival Park nobody is going to know what the
tourists are talking about when they ask for directions and
they could all end up over at the landfill or somewhere.

   Also Ice Plant Island is something just about everybody can pronounce correctly even if they are from Ahia
or New Jersey. The tourists have enough trouble already
with names like Wanchese and Manteo and Chicamacomico and Bodie Island without creating another problem for
them.

   Uncle Jack thinks the tourists should be able to
enjoy their vacations without having to worry about how to
pronounce something every time they turn around.

   Also Uncle Jack has never heard of any other
place in the world that has an Ice Plant Island and as far
as he is concerned that should be enough reason not to

---

* NOTE: Ultimately it would be renamed Roanoke Festival Park.

change it. "Ireland" probably sounded like a pretty dumb name for an island at one time but the Irish people stuck to it and now many people from all over the world like to go there on their vacations. If you ask Uncle Jack there is a lesson there for all of us.

Conservatively,
Uncle Jack

Build It and They Will Come

Dear Uncle Jack,

I have been reading a lot about how the people who own all those big houses up in Corolla want the state to build a bridge across from the Currituck County mainland to the Outer Banks. They say it will help relieve traffic congestion and also help to get people out of there in case of a hurricane. Do you think they ought to build a bridge up there, Uncle Jack?

Lorna Dune
Kitty Hawk

Dear Lorna,

Uncle Jack is glad you asked him about this because he has been thinking about traffic a lot lately, mostly while waiting to make left turns on the Bypass but other times, too, like the other day when he drove to Norfolk and saw the cars in the southbound lanes of Highway 158 backed up bumper-to-bumper from Kitty Hawk all the way back to Grandy.

If you want to know the truth he was a little surprised to see that traffic jam up in Currituck County because he thought it was supposed to be a thing of the past since they made the highway five lanes all the way to Norfolk and doubled the size of the Wright Brothers bridge.

Back in the '70s before he moved here he would have to crawl through the gauntlet of Currituck County pig farms on two-lane Highway 158 and creep across Currituck Sound on the old two-lane bridge and he could hardly wait until they widened the road and built the new bridge so he could breeze right on down to Nags Head at a steady 50 mph.

In those days there wasn't even a stoplight at Duck Road because hardly anybody except real estate speculators ever wanted to go up that way because there was nothing up there except huge tracts of empty land from the ocean to the sound.

He knows exactly how those people feel who want a new bridge across the sound up north because it will save them a lot of aggravation, especially on weekends when the rental houses change over. He can even imagine that for a couple of years after the new bridge opens they will think they have died and gone to heaven before reality sets in again and the southbound traffic to the new bridge starts to back up somewhere near Williamsburg, Virginia. Then the clamor will begin to "four-lane" the bridge which will take another ten years and eventually bring another brief respite before gridlock sets in again.

In the meantime traffic will have steadily increased on the Bypass and pressure will mount to construct a 30-mile-long overpass (probably to be called the Uberbypass) on top of the existing five-lane Highway 158 through Kitty Hawk, Kill Devil Hills and Nags Head (which will probably be renamed the Marc Basnight Memorial Service Road), all of which will connect to the new (two-lane) Bonner Bridge to Greater Metropolitan Hatteras.**

Anyway, to answer your question, Uncle Jack thinks they will have to build a bridge across Currituck Sound some day. In the short run it will solve a problem and in the long run compound it, just like every other traffic "improvement" they have made around here in the last 30 years. (Can you believe that in 1970 there was only one stoplight in all of Dare County?)

If you want to know the truth Uncle Jack does not think there is any solution to the traffic problem on the Outer Banks. It will continue to get worse as the years go by and there is not much anybody can do about it except Mother Nature who could decide to wipe the slate clean one of these days.

The bottom line is that if visitors keep coming to the Outer Banks in droves they are going to have to learn to put up with most of the same aggravating problems they came here to escape. And those of us who live here will have to do the same.

Fatalistically,
Uncle Jack

P.S. You don't have to wait for the new bridge to open to make some money. You could go out on Highway 158 any Saturday or Sunday afternoon and peddle Prozac car-to-car to the folks who are parked out there waiting to make the left turn up to Duck.

** NOTE: Uncle Jack came close. It was the Marc Basnight Bridge that ultimately would replace the Bonner Bridge.

(OBX)

Mr. Bobby Jim Hunter of Clod, North Carolina, is shown fishing from the roof of his $50,000 4WD Toyota pickup after the tide came in at Hatteras Point Wednesday. The treacherous Hatteras surf ("Graveyard of ORVs") has claimed more than 400 AWD cars and trucks since 1970. The CB antennas of many early victims can be seen at low tide, waving in silvery counterpoint to the golden sea oats which fringe the nearby dunes. (Photo courtesy Dare County Tourist Bureau.)

Here Comes the Judge

If you ask Uncle Jack one of the best things about living in a country like the U.S.A. is that almost everybody has a chance to be somebody when he grows up. You do not have to be born rich and you do not have to have a father who is a commissioner or some other important person like that.

All you have to do is go to school and pay attention to the teacher and learn how to do those arithmetic problems where the trains start out from different places and also memorize the capitals of all the states and if you can do this you are almost sure to be a success. If you can manage to hang around long enough to graduate from high school there is almost no limit on how far you can go. Uncle Jack knows.

He has been thinking a lot this week about how lucky he was to be born in the U.S.A. because something happened to him this week that would never happen to an ordinary, run-of-the-mill person in most other countries. What happened was that Uncle Jack was picked to be a judge of the Nags Head Surf Fishing Tournament which starts today and goes until Saturday.

In case you do not know what this means Uncle Jack will explain that the judges are people who drive up and down the beach for two days, picking up dead fish and measuring them so the scorers can figure out who won the tournament. He should not have to explain that this is a very important job and not everybody can get to be a judge. For one thing, you have to be highly respected in your community and for another thing you have to own a four-wheel-drive vehicle, but Uncle Jack is not sure which is most important. All he knows is that as soon as he bought his new secondhand Jeep they picked him to be a judge, no questions asked.

Anyway, this is the highest honor Uncle Jack has ever had and he can hardly believe that it has happened. Who could have guessed that an ordinary, run-of-the-mill child of poor parents, born in the north woods of Wisconsin thousands of miles from the nearest ocean, would one day grow up to be a Judge of the oldest, largest, and finest surf fishing tournament in Dare County?

If you ask Uncle Jack this is real proof that the American way of life is working just like Thomas Jefferson said it would.

Uncle Jack is not taking this honor lightly, either. He is doing his best to get ready so he will be able to do a good job of judging. For one thing he has sworn off all forms of spiritual beverages until after the judging is over because he knows how hard it is to measure fish if your hands are shaking or when you have impaired your faculties with foreign substances such as Molson's ale or Heineken's beer.

He knows he has to measure every fish very carefully because the outcome of the whole tournament could rest on how well he does his measuring. Also he knows he could be assaulted by some irate fisherman if he does it wrong.

Uncle Jack knows that different types of fish get different numbers of points so he is studying hard to learn the various kinds of fish so he does not make any mistakes that way. Yesterday he finally mastered most of the main differences between the tarpon and the flounder and he plans to keep studying right up to the time the judging starts.

Uncle Jack does want to warn all the contestants about the new state law they passed a few weeks ago that says you cannot drink beer or any other spiritual beverages in a motor vehicle even when the motor vehicle is on the beach and not on the highway.

He wants all the contestants to know that he is planning to keep a sharp eye out for anybody who breaks this law and he will not hesitate to report them to the police. As far as Uncle Jack is concerned beer drinking has no place in the Nags Head Surf Fishing Tournament anyway and he knows the vast majority of the club members will back him up on that.

Anyway it is a real honor for Uncle Jack to serve as a judge and he hopes he will do a good enough job so they will ask him again next year.

P.S. He is only kidding about the beer drinking.
P.P.S. God Bless America.

"They weren't lying, Gert! You CAN see it from here!"

Advice
for Houseguests

Uncle Jack has lived on the Outer Banks for a long time now and he has noticed some very interesting things about the flora and fauna. One thing he has noticed is that there are lots of swans around here in the winter but hardly any in the summer.

Another thing he has noticed is that houseguests are just the opposite of swans. You hardly ever see a houseguest around here in the winter but they are all over the place in the summer. Come to think of it Uncle Jack has never seen a houseguest and a swan at the same time.

Uncle Jack has noticed that the average houseguest tends to be a lot more trouble than the average swan. Swans eat out most of the time for one thing, and they never take showers. Houseguests spend most of their time sitting around the dining room table waiting for food to appear when they are not in the bathroom.

Anyway Uncle Jack thought it would be a good idea to give some advice to houseguests who are planning to come to the Outer Banks. These suggestions are not "cast in concrete" as they say over at Coastal Redi-Mix. Not everybody likes Stilton cheese, for instance, so you might not have to bring any if you are not staying with Uncle Jack.

What to bring your host and hostess: One half-gallon Rebel Yell bourbon per person (excluding children under 5), three cases Rolling Rock beer, six pounds medium shrimp (heads off, please), two dozen steamed jumbo jimmy crabs, two dozen clams, five pounds scallops, three dozen Silver Queen corn, one bushel Currituck peaches, three pounds Stilton cheese, two cases good imported red table wine (ditto white), two loaves French bread, five pounds Virginia Diner peanuts.

Also bring assorted non-perishable items such as canned truffles and caviar that your host and hostess can enjoy next winter while watching the swans. Also bring sheets, pillow cases, towels, soap, deodorant, toothpaste, shampoo, depilatories, aspirin, insect spray, styrofoam coolers and good books, all of which you should remember to forget when you leave.

Chores your host and hostess should not have to do during your visit: cook meals, wash dishes, take out garbage, clean bathtub, scratch dogs, mow lawn, make morning coffee, smile.

Things you can do to express appreciation to your host and hostess: Go to see *The Lost Colony* every night by yourselves. Talk about pleasant things like what you are planning to fix for dinner tomorrow night or where you are planning to take your host and hostess for lunch. Do not talk about the horrible traffic or how the developers are ruining the Outer Banks or how rotten the fishing is in the summer or how terrible the weather has been during your visit.

Your host and hostess do not want to have to tell you how wonderful the weather was last week, how great the fishing is in the spring and fall, or how easy it is to cross the Bypass in February.

If you do everything Uncle Jack has suggested your host and hostess might invite you to come back again. If you are really lucky they might ask you to come back next winter when the swans are here.

CROAKER RECIPE
(From *Uncle Jack's Outer Banks Cookbook*)

One medium croaker, unscaled, head on
One cup crushed bran flakes
Three tablespoons cod liver oil
One cup crushed ice
Four ounces cognac

Roll croaker in bran flakes until well coated. Fry in cod liver oil, three minutes on each side. Remove from pan and set aside. Pour cognac over crushed ice. Drink cognac while waiting for croaker to cool. When croaker has reached room temperature, feed to cat. (Cats like croaker; Uncle Jack does not.)

Swimmers in Nags Head enjoy watching the antics of board riders when the "surf's up." Surfing is prohibited between the hours of 10 a.m. and 4 p.m. but the high-spirited youngsters often forget the time in their excited search for the "perfect wave."

The Adventures of Uncle Jack

Surfing, of a Sort

These past seven days have been flawless: one sunny, warm, dry, windless day after another. It is ten o'clock on a Sunday morning and Uncle Jack is well into his fourth hour of staring out to sea from the upper deck on his house in South Nags Head.

For the first hour it was just him and the pelicans who are without doubt the most entertaining creatures on the planet with the possible exception of politicians. Whether these birds are simply flying by, skimming the wave tops as they are wont to do, or dive-bombing for their breakfasts as they are doing this morning, Uncle Jack can think of few things that are more fun to watch than pelicans doing whatever they happen to be doing.

Time has passed, however, and he and the pelicans are no longer alone. For the past half hour he has been watching the struggles of a hapless surfer whose ineptitude on the long board is exceeded only by that of Uncle Jack himself. He is reminded of the day some 45 years ago at Waikiki Beach when he rented his first and only surfboard—a mammoth slab of mahogany weighing perhaps 200 pounds. (Fiberglass was still just a gleam in the eye of Mr. Dow and Mr. Corning.)

It took him an hour to paddle out to the first row of breakers, where he spent another hour trying to stand upright on the board for more than a mil-

 # The Lost Colony

Dear Uncle Jack,

I've heard so many stories about what happened to the Lost Colony that I don't now what to believe any more. What really happened to the Lost Colony, Uncle Jack?

Confused,
Corolla

Dear Confused,

The Lost Colony is a good example of why people shouldn't believe everything some developer tells them. Sir Walter Raleigh's brochures were full of hype about the "terrifick fishing" and the "salubrious climate" in this "goodliest soile under the cope of heaven." But Raleigh never said a word about the mosquitoes on

lisecond. He finally gave up and allowed the board and himself to drift back to the beach which is what he should have done in the first place because it was a very pleasant experience.

Unfortunately, he washed ashore nearly a mile from the rental place to which he had to drag his mahogany albatross, which took another hour for which he had to pay. And that was the inglorious beginning and end of his surfing career.

(OBX)

Roanoke Island.

He lured those poor colonists over here about 200 years before Sir Reginald Off invented insect spray and those nasty little buggers nearly ate them alive before they decided to split.

Uncle Jack agrees with Professor Hermann von Schitzlinger of Harvard who says the colonists just packed up and went to Illinois one day after somebody told them there weren't any bugs up there. According to Schitzlinger the word "Croatan" was carved on a tree by some illiterate colonist who didn't know how to spell Chicago.

The professor even says he found some direct descendants of the Lost Colony still living in Highland Park, a suburb of Chicago. He knows they were from the Outer Banks because they pronounce it "Hoighland Pork." And now you know.

Historically,
Uncle Jack

Riding Out a Hurricane ... Was That It?

Uncle Jack's Hurricane Bonnie journal:

Tuesday, Aug. 25, 6 a.m. National Weather Service puts Bonnie several hundred miles south of Cape Hatteras and moving north-northwest at 6 miles per hour. Dare County officials order immediate mandatory evacuation. Uncle Jack, having calculated in his head without the aid of sophisticated digital instrumentation that it will take upwards of two days for Bonnie to reach Hatteras, goes to work instead of to Greenville.

Tuesday, Aug. 25, 6 p.m. Latest advisory puts Bonnie several hundred miles south of Hatteras and still creeping north-northwest at 6 miles an hour. Uncle Jack sits on his deck from which he has a a splendid view of hundreds of cars sitting bumper-to-bumper on the Washington Baum Bridge, providing Wednesday morning's front-page photo in hundreds of newspapers

"The relatively placid seas and those vacationers behind me notwithstanding, Dan, it's really starting to blow out here."

across the country—a refreshing change from Monica Lewinsky.

Tuesday, Aug. 25, 10 p.m. Uncle Jack is awakened from sound sleep by someone banging on his front door. It is an intense lady from Dare County Emergency Management urging him to evacuate immediately or face dire consequences. Knowing that Bonnie is still nearly two days south of Cape Hatteras and moving north at 6 miles an hour, Uncle Jack thanks her for her concern and goes back to bed, suggesting that she do the same.

Wednesday, Aug. 26, 6 a.m. Now completely alone in their neighborhood (except for the Emergency Management people who stop by frequently to utter cries of alarm) Uncle Jack and Mrs. Uncle Jack eat breakfast on the deck where they have a splendid view of large combers rolling sideways onto the beach—the only visible indication that there is any weather of any kind within a thousand miles of Nags Head. Still no wind and no rain. No tourists, either, so Uncle Jack decides to stay home and catch up on paperwork while occasionally consulting The Weather Channel. He quickly calculates that he is down about $1,500 while Bonnie is still floundering around 200 miles south of Cape Lookout.

Wednesday, Aug. 26, noon. Wind has finally begun to pick up so Uncle Jack stows the deck furniture and goes inside to a sumptuous lunch of leftover osso bucco washed down with two pints of Guinness. At 2 p.m. he is awakened from a richly deserved post-prandial nap by loud banging at front door. This time it is a Nags Head policeman urging him to evacuate immediately and informing him that water service to South Nags Head would be cut off soon. In his sleep-deprived state Uncle Jack accepts this information gracefully, knowing he will not need water as long as his Guinness holds out. He estimates it is a four-month supply.

Wednesday, Aug. 26, evening. Wind continues to freshen with gusts occasionally reaching 15 miles an hour. Long-broken latch on Uncle Jack's screen door comes back to haunt him as the door flies open and bangs against the wall for a few minutes until he nails it shut. Uncle Jack sleeps like a baby in his own bed, secure in the knowledge that Bonnie is still churning around somewhere south of Wilmington. Emergency Management people seem to have given up on him and are ready to let him die a horrible death if that is what he chooses to do. Uncle Jack applauds their decision.

Thursday, Aug. 27, 6 p.m. Can it be over? The rain stops, the wind drops off to nothing and Uncle Jack decides to drive up and feed the cats at his gallery. No sign of damage anywhere. No sign of cats, either. Presumably, they heeded the mandatory evacuation.

Friday, Aug. 28, 3 a.m. Bonnie is back! Uncle Jack is awakened by banging screen door, which finally slams itself shut so tightly it stays shut without Uncle Jack's intervention. Rain lashes the windows and his house shakes under wind gusts that could conceivably have reached 50 miles an hour.

Friday, Aug. 29, 10 a.m. Uncle Jack drives up the Beach Road again to see if he can find any cats to feed. Still no signs of significant damage except for the Nags Head Inn sign, which now hangs at an odd angle, no doubt the victim of incipient rust that weakens all things oceanfront over time. Uncle Jack's driveway is littered with 20-year-old shingles from his gallery roof. He makes mental note that he is going to have to do something about that roof one of these days.

And that's the way it went. Once again, Uncle Jack is glad that he is not a member of the Dare County Emergency Management Team, who have to make what could be life-or-death decisions on the basis of insufficient information only to have people like Uncle Jack poke fun at them. He knows that they meant well and he wishes them well in their future lifesaving efforts.

He offers his sympathy to all those who were not as lucky as he was.

But the fact remains that once again thousands of people, visitors and locals alike, have endured the agony of evacuation when they would have been better off browsing in Uncle Jack's gallery for four days.

There really isn't anyone for Uncle Jack to be mad at but Mother Nature, however, and who can stay mad at Mother Nature very long when you live on the Outer Banks which is one of her creations.

The Adventures of Uncle Jack

Proud to Be
a Quitter

Most of the people who don't smoke must have a hard time understanding why smokers smoke when even the dumb smokers who never finished high school must have heard by now that smoking is bad for their health.

Some of the non-smokers probably tried to learn how to smoke when they were young but it made them sick right off the bat instead of having to wait thirty years to get lung cancer. They were lucky.

Uncle Jack does not smoke but it isn't hard for him to understand why people do smoke even though they know it makes them cough and it stinks up their clothes and it is costing them a fortune. Uncle Jack knows why they smoke because a long time ago he used to smoke, too, and he can remember what it was like. For ten years he started every day with a cigarette and in between he smoked at least twenty more, two or three of which he really enjoyed.

This is not something Uncle Jack is proud of. It is not easy to admit that he was a slave but for ten years Uncle Jack belonged to the Marlboro Man. One day Uncle Jack got really fed up with the Marlboro Man and decided he would never smoke a cigarette again. He knows exactly when this was because it was on the very day his only begotten son was born. (Uncle Jack has always had a flair for the dramatic.)

Actually Uncle Jack had tried to quit smoking many times before but the Marlboro Man wouldn't let him. This time, though, Uncle Jack had help from Bob Newhart.

Back in the old days Bob Newhart was a stand-up comedian who did funny sets where he would pretend he was talking on the phone to somebody. In one of those skits he pretended to be a high-pressure salesman in England who was talking to Sir Walter Raleigh.

Part of an actual advertisement from the R.J. Reynolds Tobacco Co. for Prince Albert tobacco. It urged: "Take a tip from Sir Walt. ... If he hadn't been willing to take a chance four hundred years ago, he never would have known what a smoke was like."

Raleigh has just discovered tobacco in America and he is trying to convince this salesman that there is big money to be made in making something called "cigarettes" from tobacco, which he tries to describe over the phone but the listener is skeptical: "It has a lot of different uses, like, what are some of the uses, Walt?… 'You can shred it up … and put it in a piece of paper.' Ha ha ha. 'And roll it up.' Ha ha ha …," the salesman says, laughing. "Don't tell me, Walt, don't tell me: You stick it in your ear, right? Ha! Ha! Ha!…Oh: 'Between your lips!'…

"Then what do you do, Walt?" The salesman is laughing uncontrollably now. After he recovers, he says, " 'You set fire to it!' Ha ha ha! …Then what do you do, Walt?…

"'You inhale the smoke,' huh? Ha! Ha! Ha!…"

Anyway Uncle Jack has not smoked a cigarette since November 2, 1961, and he cannot even begin to figure out how much money he has not spent on cigarettes but it must have been enough to pay for all the bourbon he has consumed in the same period. We are talking real money here.

He would like to conclude by saying that he would be happy to serve as an inspiration to anybody who would like to quit smoking. If somebody as inherently spineless as Uncle Jack can quit, he is sure that anybody can.

And if all else fails he will let you borrow his Bob Newhart record.

Days of Yours

Uncle Jack was thinking the other day that he has been around here so long now he could legitimately call himself an old-timer. Not a real old-timer like some of the older natives but maybe some sort of senior level carpetbagger at least. Anyway, he has been letting his mind wander back over the 37 years since he crossed the Currituck bridge and drove down the Bypass for the first time.

He cannot remember exactly how many buildings were already beginning to clutter up the Bypass in 1969 but there weren't very many. The only ones he can remember for sure are the ABC store and the Sportsman's Diner which was about the only restaurant in town, especially in the winter which in those days lasted from Labor Day to about the middle of June.

There was no stoplight at the main intersection at Colington Road then because when the DOT installed one of those car counters it rusted out before it had counted 100 cars. The first 7-Eleven was still a gleam in some accountant's eye over at the Southland Corporation and all the gourmet food lovers used to line up at the Trading Post when the Pepperidge Farm truck came in from Norfolk on Fridays.

The Kentucky Fried Chicken at Whalebone Junction was the only franchise food place and if you were really lucky you would not have to wait in line more than 30 minutes to get your order which gave new meaning to the term "fast food."

The Nags Head Town Hall was that little white building across from Jockey's Ridge where they keep a small fire truck now. It was big enough because the town only had one policeman to handle the drunk drivers (which is what they called them in those days) and one clerk to answer the phone and collect the taxes. She did not have much to do either because the town taxes didn't amount to much. Uncle Jack remembers when he could pay his out of petty cash and still have enough left over for a piece of Mrs. Hayman's lemon chess pie at the Arlington Hotel.

Those were the days when Duck was still at the end of the earth and South Nags Head was about to be ravished by a horde of developers. He remembers when they built that strange domed Bucky Fuller house way down at the end of South Nags Head and how wide the beach was in front of it and how fast that beach disappeared and left those domes sort of hanging in mid-air. It was not much more than ten years from start to finish as he recalls.

That was when developers started carving South Nags Head up into little lots of running north and south instead of deep lots running east and west from the ocean to the road. This was a very smart thing to do but only if you were in the business of selling lots. It was not so smart, though, if you are one of the people who is now watching his expensive oceanfront lot vanish from under his expensive ocean-front house which he cannot move back because some peasant built his shack on the cheap lot behind him.

Uncle Jack remembers lots of hurricanes from Ginger in 1970 right up to Isabel and what they did to South Nags Head where he has lived for the past 15 years or so. He has to wonder how anybody who has lived here for a few years can seriously talk about something called "erosion control" much less want to spend countless millions of dollars trying to achieve it.

"Erosion control" sounds like it belongs in the same category with "military intelligence" and "computer literacy"—ideas that self-destruct when you think about them. You can believe that "erosion control" is possible and you can spend endless amounts of money trying to prove it but it always seems to be a few million dollars ahead of you. At least it seems that way to Uncle Jack and he has been around here watching the ocean for a while.

For a lot less money the commissioners could put up some nice signs at the end of each bridge leading to the Outer Banks and on the signs they could put a message something like this: "WARNING! You are entering an unstable barrier island which is known to shift around a lot when the wind blows. BUILD AT YOUR OWN RISK!"

Uncle Jack is smart enough to know that signs like that would not keep some people from building whatever the law allows as close to the ocean as they can put it, but in the long run they could save the tax-payers a pile of money about the size of Jockey's Ridge.

OBX

Uncle Jack Knows

Yo, Grad! Listen Up

Uncle Jack would like to take this opportunity to congratulate all those young persons who will graduate from high school this month. As far as he is concerned graduating from high school is one of life's crowning achievements and he only regrets that so many young men and women fall by the wayside, never to know what it means to reach the pinnacle.

For as Uncle Jack knows it is the high school graduates who become the movers and shakers, the captains of industry, the leaders in every walk of life. For them and them alone are reserved the Mercedes Benzes, the Lincoln Town Cars and the Range Rovers of the future. What it boils down to is that if you can survive high school without going completely bonkers there is probably nothing in life that can stop you from achieving your goals with the possible exception of early pregnancy.

Uncle Jack has been ruminating a lot about high school this week because he got a call from an old friend in his home town inviting him to attend the 50th annual reunion of his high school gradua-tion class this summer. He has never gone to a high school reunion before but he has decided to go this year because his friend said it might be the last one. There were only 100 people in Uncle Jack's class to begin with and apparently they have been dropping like flies in recent years, many of them as a result of bad habits they picked up in high school such as drinking and smoking and ambition.

Anyway he has been trying to think of some good advice he could give today's high school graduates now that he has been out in the real world for half a century. Unfortunately he has not come up with any-thing worth mentioning except "if you haven't started smoking don't start, and if you have, quit now"—but you do not have to be a high school graduate to give good advice like that.

Just about everything he could say about how to live your life already has been covered pretty well by bumper stickers such as "Save the Whales," "I'd Rather Be in Hatteras" and "Hug Your Kid Today" (which he hopes you will save for later).

If you want to know the truth everything is changing so fast today that he is afraid that most of the advice he would give you would be wrong and you would wind up as poor as he is.

On the other hand if you wound up as happy as he is that would not be so bad. And he can tell you for sure that you do not have to have a lot of money to be happy and also that a lot of people who do have a lot of money are not very happy.

As far as he is concerned the best situation you can be in is to have a lot of money and be very happy at the same time but he has not figured out how to do that himself so he is not very much help in that department.

Anyway Uncle Jack is very proud of each and every one of you who will receive a high school diploma this month and he hopes you will cherish it enough to want to take it to the framing shop of your choice and have it expensively matted and framed so you can be proud to hang it on the wall in your office at the Burger King or your cubicle in the county office building or wherever you happen to wind up working.

And if you need assistance finding a good framer Uncle Jack will be more than happy to help. He firmly believes that high school graduates should stick together.

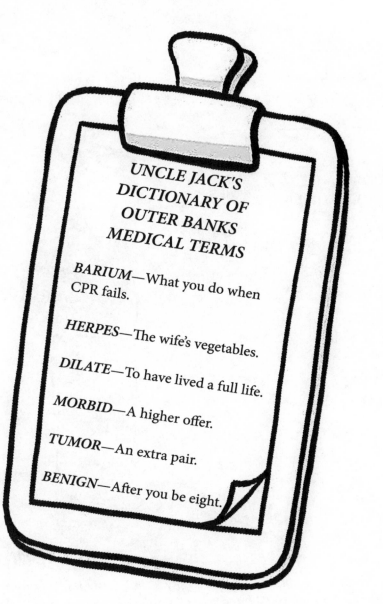

UNCLE JACK'S
DICTIONARY OF
OUTER BANKS
MEDICAL TERMS

BARIUM—What you do when CPR fails.

HERPES—The wife's vegetables.

DILATE—To have lived a full life.

MORBID—A higher offer.

TUMOR—An extra pair.

BENIGN—After you be eight.

"I'm sorry, sir, but Dostoyevsky is not considered summer reading. I'll have to ask you to come with me."

Uncle Jack's Dare County Crime Roundup

Southern Shores, Jan. 14—A rash of burglaries has angered residents of this quiet residential community. Police attribute the upsurge of crime to a recent announcement by state officials that Southern Shores is the wealthiest town in North Carolina.

"How long is it going to take these dumb crooks to find out we're just as poor as everybody else in Dare County?" asked Carter Van Trumpington, a retired bank janitor who moved to Southern Shores from Akron, Ohio, two years ago.

Van Trumpington's modest 12-room bungalow on Dogwood Trail was one of four homes to be burglarized last Wednesday. "They are smart enough to come on Wednesday when we're all down at the C&B for Senior Citizens' Day," Van Trumpington admitted ruefully.

"They took everything," he complained. "Our Kmart 19-inch black-and-white TV, the wife's best set of Ginzu knives, the bamboo steamer, my old snow tires from when we lived in Akron, both sets of golf clubs. We are destitute."

Town officials vowed to continue their fight to restore the community's tarnished image. "If we're so rich how come we're the only town in Dare County where the council still has to meet in the firehouse?" one councilman asked reporters, somewhat rhetorically.

* * *

Nags Head, Jan. 12—Nags Head police arrested two young commercial fishermen last night following a contretemps at the Crafty Tavern on the (CONT. NEXT PAGE)

Crime

(FROM PREV. PAGE)

causeway. According to Lt. Ronnie Pickens of the NHPD, the fracas erupted when Filmore Pullup, 22, of Clam Quarter, attacked Joe Bob Crammit, 20, of Drainfield after Crammit allegedly accused him of cheating at chess.

Witnesses said the two men, who had returned earlier in the day from a successful two-week fishing trip on the trawler *Spirit of Stumpy Point*, had been quietly playing chess and drinking Diet Pepsi for several hours when Pullup suddenly struck Crammit in the face with a copy of *Contemporary Poetry Review*, which he had concealed in his bait cooler.

Friends of the combatants said the fight had been brewing for more than a week at sea during which the men, both high school graduates, had quarreled over everything from the artistic validity of non-objectivist painting to the usefulness of Kant's categorical imperative as a guide to correct moral behavior.

One shipmate said Pullup had refused to speak to Crammit for several days after the latter allegedly oversalted the crew's luncheon bouillabaisse.

After reading two pages of *Contemporary Poetry Review*, police charged Pullup with assault with a deadly weapon.

* * *

Manteo, Jan. 10— Daring thieves have kidnapped a statue of Sir Walter Raleigh from a downtown Manteo park and are holding it for ransom, police reported today. While no witnesses to the crime have come forward, authorities believe it must have occurred sometime during the weekend.

"Sir Walter was there when I rolled up the sidewalks Friday night," said Manteo street department employee Art Withbeck, "but when I came in Monday morning he was gone."

The colossal Raleigh sculpture, carved from a single enormous cypress log, has attracted flocks of tourists and woodpeckers to downtown Manteo in recent years, but has thus far failed to win universal acclaim as a major work of art.

Police have refused to reveal the contents of a ransom note found at the scene of the crime, but the *Current* has learned from a reliable source that the kidnappers have promised never to return the statue if the town council will agree to pay them $5,000 in small, unmarked bills.

Town officials deny that they engineered the kidnapping as part of Manteo's beautification program for the forthcoming Quadricentennial celebrations. However, one councilman, who did not wish to be identified, said that he thought the $5,000 demand was a "steal."

"We shall not rest until we have brought the perpetrators of this heinous crime to the bar of justice," a police official said this morning, repeating almost exactly the words of a local art critic at the unveiling of the statue several years ago.

OBX

Let the
Monitor Lie

Uncle Jack has a good friend named O'Brien who lives up in New Jersey where you can get the *New York Times* delivered every day if you want to. This has never seemed to Uncle Jack to be a good enough reason to live in New Jersey but O'Brien seems to think it is and Uncle Jack is glad about that because whenever an article about the Outer Banks appears in the *New York Times* O'Brien clips it out and sends it to him.

This is good because the *New York Times* tells you everything you could possibly want to know about something and then some and you always get a fresh perspective on the subject no matter how much you thought you knew about it. This week O'Brien sent a clipping about the wreck of the Civil War ship called the *Monitor*, which sank in a storm off Hatteras at the very end of 1862.

The reason the *New York Times* is writing about the *Monitor* now is that various "experts" are

saying it is now or never if we want to salvage the
wreckage and get it into a museum someplace where
people can stare at it in comfort instead of risking
their lives to dive down 223 feet in a rubber suit to
stare at it.

The experts say it would cost about $50 mil-
lion to bring up all the pieces that are left but it would
only cost about $22 million to bring up the propeller
and the turret which are about the only things rec-

ognizable after 130 years of damage from saltwater and fishermen's nets and maybe even a depth charge or two during World War II.

Uncle Jack was in the Navy and knows that with the sonar they had in those days it would be easy to mistake the wreck of the *Monitor* for a German submarine or even a large tuna.

Anyway, it is not easy to raise $50 million or even $22 million to do something that is not going to make a lot of money for somebody so the people who want to salvage the wreckage are trying to make the *Monitor* sound like it is the most important ship ever built and that it would be a crime against civilization not to spend a paltry $22 million or whatever to haul it up.

One man who wrote a book about the *Monitor* went so far as to say that when it comes to being important the *Monitor* is "on the level with the Wright brothers' airplane," which is funny enough to make Uncle Jack wonder if he shouldn't be the main speaker at the next meeting of the Man Will Never Fly Society. The same author suggests that maybe the U.S. Navy should put up most of the money because of its pride in its "high-tech history," which suggests to Uncle Jack that he doesn't know as much about the Navy as he should.

Uncle Jack spent most of his waking hours while he was in the Navy reading Samuel Eliot Morison's *History of U.S. Naval Operations in World War II* from which he concluded that the less said about "high-tech operations" the better—including dropping depth charges on the *Monitor* which was perfectly capable of falling apart without any help from the Navy.

If you ask Uncle Jack it would be better to let sleeping turrets lie and spend money on something really worthwhile like moving the Hatteras Lighthouse to the moon, and eventually to Mars if the Park Service can scrape up the money. (OBX)

True Bravery

Dear Uncle Jack,

Me and my girl friend were having an argument at Sam and Omie's the other night about who was the bravest person who ever lived. She said it was some broad I never heard of called Amelia Airhard and I said it was Evil Knievel. Tell her she's full of avocado dip, Uncle Jack.

Pool Shark,
Nags Head

Dear Shark,

You were both wrong. The bravest person who ever lived was the first one who had the guts to eat a raw oyster.

Snottily,
Uncle Jack

A Great Summer ... In Spite of the Wonderful Weather

Uncle Jack is pleased to report that he has made it halfway through the summer and he is holding up OK. The way he feels right now he thinks he can get through to Labor Day without suffering a total physical and mental breakdown, which is always a possibility when you operate a business on the Outer Banks.

So far his cash flow is pretty good in spite of the seemingly endless sunny weather, which has enabled our tourist visitors to spend an inordinate amount of time on the beach and has cut seriously into their shopping time. He can remember only two rainy days in the past six weeks, which could be disastrous for businesses like Uncle Jack's but it has not been, so he is happy the tourists are having such a good time.

Right now it looks as if he will reach his major financial goal, which is to make enough money by Labor Day to pay off the bank for the money they lent him last winter so they will let him borrow some more to get through next winter. Sometimes Uncle Jack feels more like a sharecropper than a shopkeeper but he knows it goes with the territory and he would rather be here than anywhere else he can think of so he is not complaining.

One of the nicest things about being a shopkeeper for such a long time (this is his 29th year in Nags Head) is that he gets to renew his acquaintance with so many nice people from all over who have been coming into his shop for as many years as he has had it.

He has watched the same toddlers who once threatened to lay waste to his entire inventory grow up to be doctors and lawyers and computer programmers and other forms of solvent adults—all with a highly developed appreciation for expensive antique prints and maps. He has to confess that there were times when he wanted to kill them but it does prove that in business it is a good idea to think of what is best in the long term.

The downside of being in business so long and getting old and senile at the same time is that with ever greater frequency he cannot remember the names of people whose faces he recognizes being they have been in his shop maybe 50 times and spent enough money to send his children through college.

He always feels bad about this and he would like to take this opportunity to offer his annual apology to all of these wonderful people and to thank them for being kind enough to tell him who they are when they notice the look of total panic on Uncle Jack's face.

It is always fun to reminisce with his customers about the old days on the Outer Banks 25 or 30 years ago when the Tourist Bureau used to call it "A Secret Worth Keeping," which Uncle Jack still thinks deserves a prize for the oddest slogan ever dreamed up by a tourist bureau.

Some of his customers can remember when his gallery started out in a little building at the First Colony Inn when it was on the oceanfront across from Jimmy Austin's seafood store. One day the brakes let go on a large fish truck parked at Austin's and it rolled down and smashed into Uncle Jack's old gallery, with devastating results.

Fortunately, he knew that this was bound to happen sooner or later and he had moved to his new location some years before. But it does prove the truth of one of the main tenets of the Lutheran faith, which is: "Don't get too happy because there may be a runaway fish truck in your future."

The Adventures of Uncle Jack

Truly
a Tire-Changing
Experience

Uncle Jack had to drive to Norfolk Friday to take his California grandchildren and their parents to the airport. He has made this trip a hundred times in the last 30 years without mishap but not this time.

God had apparently decided that it was his turn to have a flat tire.

Lucky for him and his passengers it happened in the parking lot at the Crawford House restaurant in Currituck County and not at 60 miles an hour somewhere along Route 168 where the annual death toll has already reached alarming proportions in recent years.

He quickly called his erstwhile friends at the AARP Automobile Club only to learn that the nearest road service purveyor was in a town called Kill Devil Hills, North Carolina—which the operator thought was hilarious for some reason—and that it would take at least two hours for help to arrive.

After a brief, lugubrious period of contemplation, Uncle Jack and his son decided to change the tire themselves in spite of the brutal heat and humidity and their almost total collective lack of experience in the tire-changing department.

They succeeded, barely, but they learned a lot in the process, and Uncle Jack would like to pass on some tips to any of his readers who might some day find themselves in the same miserable predicament.

1. Buy a can of WD-40, put it in your car and never leave home without it. When it comes to changing tires, rust is the enemy. WD-40 is your friend.

2. Know where your tire jack is. It took Uncle Jack 20 minutes to figure out that the odd-looking lump of rusty metal attached to the inside wall of the engine compartment was in fact the jack.

3. In the absence of WD-40 try to remove as much rust as possible from the jack by banging it on the ground a few times. This act of violence will momentarily make you feel a little better even though you know the worst is still to come.

4. Remember to loosen the lug nuts before lifting the car. This will make it unnecessary for you to lower the car again after you have laboriously lifted it so that you can then loosen the lug nuts before laboriously lifting it again. Uncle Jack's only begotten son learned this the hard way, and it was not a happy experience for him. (Fortunately his wife had moved the grandchildren out of earshot long before this.)

5. Know where your spare tire is. Uncle Jack was lucky that he had actually seen his spare tire once

while having his oil changed so he had a pretty good idea where it was. Knowing where your spare tire is can be a real time saver.

6. Know how to remove your spare tire from wherever it is stored once you have found it. This turned out to be the most frustrating part of the entire procedure for Uncle Jack because there appeared to be no way of dislodging the spare from its storage space other than burning it out with an acetylene torch. Lucky for him a good Samaritan arrived at this point in his septic tank pumper truck and after sizing up the situation suggested that we consult the owner's manual which would surely tell us what we needed to know.

(Uncle Jack must confess that this was one of the most humbling moments of his life. The proud possessor of not only a high school diploma but also three degrees from various institutions of higher learning, he had been one-upped in front of his only begotten son by a humble pumper of septic tanks.)

7. Know where your owner's manual is. Again, Uncle Jack was lucky because he had never once removed it from its hiding place in the sliding compartment under the passenger seat. (Where it has now been joined by a can of WD-40.)

He sincerely hopes that none of his readers will ever have a flat tire but he also hopes that if you do, it will happen in the parking lot of the Crawford House restaurant on Route 168 in Currituck Courthouse, North Carolina. Their pre-sweetened iced tea is superb and on a hot day it takes about two gallons of it per person to change a tire. Uncle Jack knows.

OBX

Inspirational Aunt Esther

Longtime readers of Uncle Jack's column will know about his redoubtable Aunt Esther who was 79 when he started writing for the *Current* in 1980 and who celebrated her 99th birthday in March of this year. He has mentioned her many times because she was such an inspiration to him and to everyone who knew her.

He is very sorry to report that Aunt Esther passed away last week, but at the same time he is happy to tell you that her departure was quick and virtually painless—just as she hoped and prayed it would be. She continued to live independently in her own apartment until two days before her heart finally gave out, and during her brief stay in the hospital she was never without the comforting presence of friends and family. Would that all of us should be so fortunate when our time comes.

At the urging of her nieces and nephews (she never married so we were her surrogate children) she began some years ago to write down some memories of her earlier days growing up in northern Wisconsin and later teaching in the public schools in Green Bay. (Some of Uncle Jack's favorite stories involved the Green Bay Packers, some of whom she dated when she was a young teacher—back in those innocent pre-NFL days when the Packers actually worked in a meatpacking plant during the week and played football on weekends.)

Aunt Esther's last name was Sundberg rather than Sandberg and thereby hangs a tale of its own. Her mother's first husband, Uncle Jack's grandfather, was killed in an industrial accident leaving her destitute with two small children. A superb cook, she took in boarders to provide income and one of her regulars, a man named Fred Sundberg, became so enamored of her cooking that he asked Grandma Elin to marry him. Aunt Esther was their only child—and if only Uncle Jack had thought to collect a dime from every person who asked him to explain why her name was Sundberg and his was Sandberg he would be right up there with Bill Gates in the money department today.

When Aunt Esther was born in 1901, Ashland, Wisconsin, was a rough-and-tumble town full of lumberjacks and sawmill workers, many of who were single. Not surprisingly, there were brothels, one of them located in the west end (where the Sundbergs lived chastely among many other God-fearing Swedish families) and presided over by a colorful madam named Polly. Periodically, the local constabulary would "raid" Polly's establishment and her girls would be hauled off to the pokey where she would pay their fines and get them out

NEXT PAGE

to work again the same evening.

Aunt Esther often told the story about how she and her little friends would watch in awe as Polly's girls were paraded down the main street (not all of them could fit in the paddy wagon) displaying their unholy finery for all to see.

Esther and her little friends called their elegant silk garments "swishy skirts" and attempted to emulate them by inserting newspaper under their own dresses to acquire the "swishy" sound of the originals. When asked by her mother what they were doing, Aunt Esther replied that they were practicing so they could be like Polly's girls when they grew up.

Luckily for all of us, Aunt Esther survived the ensuing tongue-lashing and lived to provide us with many more stories that will be told and retold as long as she is remembered, which is likely to be a very long time.

Always, she gave more to others than she received, and Uncle Jack does believe that was one of the secrets of her long and happy life—that and her Swedish rye bread and a wonderful spiritual beverage she called the Texas Longhorn, a pitcher of which resided in her refrigerator at all times.

She will be missed.

Aunt Esther's Swedish Rye Bread

Uncle Jack has been trying to think of a nice Christmas gift he could give to all the people who have been reading his column and writing him letters and buying his book and bringing him Mineo's pizzas from Pittsburgh this year.

Finally he said to himself, "What is it that Uncle Jack loves more than anything in the world except his jug of Rebel Yell, the Outer Banks and a few members of his family?" and right away he knew the answer. What Uncle Jack loves more than almost anything else in the world is his Aunt Esther's Swedish Rye Bread, so he decided the nicest gift he could give all his friends would be the recipe for same, and here it is:

1. Mix two packages of yeast, one teaspoon sugar, one cup warm water and 1-1/2 cups white flour into a paste and let stand.

2. Mix the following separately and well: two cups milk and one cup water, five tablespoons margarine, 3/4 cup brown sugar, 3/4 cup white sugar, 1 tablespoon salt, 1 cup white flour, 1/3 cup molasses, and 3 cups rye flour.

3. Add the yeast mixture and enough white flour to make a dough (3-4 cups). Knead about 12 minutes. Put into a large, greased bowl. Let double, then punch down and let double again. Shape into four round loaves on a baking sheet (do not use pans) and let double again. Bake at 350 degrees for about one hour.

4. Let stand for one day before eating. ...

(At Uncle Jack's house the first two loaves are usually gone about ten minutes after they come out of the oven.)

OBX

"That's not white noise. That's the ocean."

The Murmur
of the Waves

Being a high school graduate is something Uncle Jack takes fairly seriously. He always tries to eat right and keep fit and get plenty of rest so he will be in top shape if the President calls and wants his help with anything.

He also does a terrific amount of reading every day so he can keep up with all the current events that are going on in all those countries that were not even on the map when he studied current events in high school—such as Kuwait.

He is careful about what he reads, too, because he knows there are only so many hours in the day and by the time he has done his day's work and checked out all the racy movies on TV there is not a whole lot of time left to keep himself well informed.

That is why he is glad he stayed in high school all the way to graduation and got his brain sharpened to such a fine point that all he has to do is aim it at any subject and he can learn everything there is to know about it in no time.

That is also why he goes to all the trouble and expense of getting the Sunday *New York Times* every week because as far as he is concerned the *New York Times* is right up there with *Parade* magazine when it comes to keeping a person informed about current events.

If Uncle Jack wants to know something about Michael Jackson's glandular imbalances he can always find out in *Parade* but if he wants to know about more serious things like if the Moslems and Druids are still fighting there is no substitute for the Sunday *New York Times* even though he does not usually get it until Tuesday afternoon at the earliest.

Uncle Jack has learned many amazing things by reading the *New York Times* and he can tell you it is worth waiting for. Last week, for example, he saw this big advertisement for a brand new condominium they are building up in this highly advanced ocean resort called Atlantic City, New Jersey.

This is some of what it says about this new condominium which looks from the picture like it might be slightly larger than the Empire State Building:

> You awake to the murmur of the waves below.
> And the sun sparkling off the surf. It's a perfect morning for coffee on your terrace. The view of beach and boardwalk and the bay is nothing short of spectacular.
> The concierge rings you up to confirm your tickets to the show and the catering arrangements for the supper party you're hosting afterwards.
> Now the only thing to decide is whether to take a dip in the pool before your tennis date or after.
> Where are you? At home. At Ocean Club. A very private, very privileged world of luxury.
> A world whose pool, tennis court and health spa make it your own special resort. A world whose exotic shops, private clubs and restaurants give it a special excitement. A world whose available services—limousine, concierge, catering—make you and your guests feel as special as you are.

> In a city of spectaculars, Ocean Club is unique. Studio, one, two, and three-bedroom condominium residences are still to be had at prices from $180,000 to over $1,000,000 ...
>
> Located between the Golden Nugget and Tropicana Casinos.

Well you can imagine how Uncle Jack felt when he got through reading all that. He can tell you he is really ashamed that he lives in one of those old-fashioned resorts where the people are so backward they still actually swim in the ocean instead of sitting up on their terraces and listening to it murmur the way they are supposed to.

Also as far as he knows there is not one single concierge anywhere on the Outer Banks from Duck to Hatteras Village and if that is not backward he doesn't know what is. If you want to know the truth Uncle Jack called up the Dare County Public Library to find out what a concierge is and they could not even find it in the big dictionary they have over there.

So it looks to Uncle Jack like the Outer Banks has a long way to go to catch up with the more advanced resorts like Atlantic City and we are all going to have to work hard and pull together. And the first thing we have to do is get rid of all those backward laws against having tall buildings on the oceanfront. It seems fairly plain that the kind of classy people who go to advance resorts like to look at the ocean from fairly high up where they never have to worry about getting salt spray in their jacuzzis.

And isn't that what we all want deep down inside?

OBX

Concentrated Sludge

Uncle Jack saw in the paper the other day where the Town of Manteo has a used Smith and Loveless 40-inch Sludge Concentrator for sale. He is not personally in the market for a sludge concentrator right now, but he thought he should pass the information along to anybody who might have missed the advertisement. You don't get an opportunity to pick up a good sludge concentrator every day, that's for sure.

If you want to know the truth, Uncle Jack is not sure what he would do with a sludge concentrator if he was lucky enough to get one. All he can think of is that it might make a nice gift for his Congressman. They are producing some serious sludge up there in Washington these days, and a good concentrator could come in handy. A 40-incher might not be big enough to do the job, though, the way things are going in Congress.

Anyway, Uncle Jack is happy as a clam that the *Outer Banks Sentinel* is giving him another chance to write about drainage and sewage and erosion and pollution and all the other neglected topics that are near and dear to his heart because they contribute so much to the quality of life here on the Outer Banks. It has been eight years since he wrote his last column for the late *Outer Banks Current*, and he has to confess he has missed doing it more than he thought he would.

Uncle Jack has to tell you that the people who run this paper really know how to drive a hard bargain. They got him into Kelly's Tavern a few weeks ago and started giving him all the free beer he could drink, which is still a lot even though he is officially a senior citizen now. (Other parts of Uncle Jack's body have pretty much shriveled up, but his bladder is amazingly supple—probably because of all the exercise it gets.) Anyway, they wouldn't let him go to the men's room until he said he would start writing his column again, so he didn't have a whole lot of choice.

As a bona fide high school graduate from back in the days when it really meant something, he is ready to tackle tough questions on just about any subject from sewage disposal to epistemology.

What he liked most about writing his column was trying to answer deep philosophical questions like "How many Realtors does it take to replace a light bulb?" And "How many politicians does it take to replace a light bulb?" Lawyers were always asking him questions like that for some reason.

Anyway Uncle Jack has been soaking his rusty old Underwood typewriter in a bucket of WD-40 and as soon as he locates a new ribbon—probably on the black market—he will be ready to rock and roll again.

Gullability

Back when Uncle Jack was a college professor and had plenty of time on his hands he used to hang around with a lot of people who called themselves "behavioral scientists." These are folks who get paid for watching what people and animals do and then trying to make some sense out of it. They try to discover "laws" that will explain the behavior of people and animals in much the same way that the law of gravity explains why things fall down and not up.

They haven't been doing too well at finding laws. People don't even obey traffic laws much less laws of behavior but the behavioral scientists are not about to give up. They are smart folks who discovered a long time ago that studying behavior is a lot more fun than working for a living.

The federal government throws money at anything called "science" so behavioral scientists can afford to fly around to conferences in places like Acapulco and Budapest where they take a few minutes to tell each other what they don't know and then go out and eat a free dinner in the best restaurant in town. Being a behavioral scientist is not the worst thing that could happen to a person, that's for sure.

Now that he is a busy shopkeeper Uncle Jack does not have a whole lot of time to think about behavioral science but it did pop into his mind the other day, though, while he was supervising the sunset from his command post on the back porch. He saw a seagull crash dive into the sound, scoop up a clam in its beak, carry it directly to a point over his driveway, drop it on the concrete, and then swoop down to pluck the meat out of the busted shell.

Now a long time before Uncle Jack knew everything there was to know, he had to take a behavioral science course in college. In that course he was told that "man" (which in those days included women) was the only creature on earth that knew how to use tools. In fact he had read a book called "Man the Toolmaker" in which the authors went on and on about how smart people are because they use tools and how dumb animals are because they don't. They told about one scientist who insisted that he had seen a chimpanzee use a stick to reach for a mango or something on a high branch but all the other scientists laughed at him and said he must have gotten his nose too far into a jug of fermented papaya juice.

Now it should be obvious to even a really dumb behavioral scientist that what our local gulls are doing is using tools to open their clamshells. Uncle Jack's driveway is no less a tool for the gulls than

Uncle Jack's corkscrew is for Uncle Jack. To put it another way our gulls are showing intelligent behavior. They have found a clever way to get a juicy morsel of meat away from a clam who has other plans for it. Among humans this is the essence of intelligent behavior. It is sometimes called "economics."

Uncle Jack has also noticed that, like people, some gulls are smarter than others[*]. Some gulls actually appear to be feebleminded. These are the ones who drop their clams right back in the water where they promptly disappear unopened. High I.Q. gulls are the ones who carry their clams to the nearest empty parking lot where they have plenty of time to chew their food after they get it.

Average gulls, the ones who seem to make up the majority of the gull population around here, drop their clams in the middle of highway 158 where many of them, sad to say, take their last meals under the wheels of speeding trucks.

But even average gulls, while they may not be as smart as the average behavioral scientist, are obviously more intelligent than behavioral scientists have led us to believe. They deserve a lot of credit, too, for going out and hunting up their own dinners instead of living off government grants.

---

[*] Indeed, this was proved out when a 2019 *Christian Science Monitor* article cited a 1981 California study showing the heavier the shell, the less high the gulls took it. It also said a 1978 study, plotting 525 shell bombings, had found young gulls were significantly less accurate than their experienced elders. And now you know.

Outer Banks Trivia

Uncle Jack has spent a fair amount of his life trying to figure out some way to get rich and famous without working but he has not come up with anything yet and sometimes wonders if he ever will. He is not a quitter, though, so he keeps trying to think of something at all times and he usually manages to stay fairly cheerful even though he is still poor and unknown.

The only time Uncle Jack gets a little depressed is when he hears about how some other person has come up with a terrific money-making idea he should have thought of himself and how that person is getting filthy rich.

This happened to him last week when he read in the paper about this man who invented a new game called College Trivia or something like that, which is just like Trivial Pursuit except that all the questions are just like the questions they put in the SAT Test, which is what all the high school graduates take if they want to get into college.

Uncle Jack is a high school graduate, as he

might have mentioned once or twice before, and he remembers how he had to take that test and how hard the questions were and how nice it would be if you could study up for it before you took it.

It is a very hard test to study for, though, because the questions are fairly dumb for the most part and you tend to fall asleep before you get very far into your studying and that is why it was so smart for that man to put it into the form of a game.

People will enjoy almost anything if you make a game out of it, and that is why even something as stupid as football has caught on and now quite popular in some circles. The same thing is happening with the SAT Test game, which is making several people very rich and Uncle Jack very jealous.

Like he said before, though, he never gives up and it did not take take him very long to come up with a new game, which he is calling Outer Banks Trivia, and he is hoping it will catch on enough so he can make a down payment on a new secondhand Jeep or maybe even a Hummer.

So far he has only had time to think of a few questions for his new game but maybe they will give you some idea of how it will go:

1. Manteo is:
   a. More often mispronounced by tourists than Rodanthe.
   b. Less often mispronounced by tourists than Wanchese.
   c. More often mispronounced than Bodie Island.
   d. Less often mispronounced by tourists than Duck.
   e. More often ducked by tourists than mispronounced.

2. Chicamacomico is:
   a. The way a few people spell Chicamacomico.
   b. Colonel Sanders' favorite vacation spot.
   c. A Native American word meaning "two feet of water covering Highway 12."
   d. What they used to call Avon before they found out that "Chicamacomico" was too long to fit over the door of the new post office.

3. Which of the following best describes the town of Southern Shores?

   a. "The Outer Banks' best-planned, best-governed and most beautiful residential community."

   b. "Gateway to Duck."

   c. "Nine Holes and a Nap."

   d. "Pentagon-by-the-Sea."

Anyway, that's the way Uncle Jack's Outer Banks Trivia game will go and he will be happy not to have to do all the hard thinking himself. And if he does finally get rich, he promises to spread his wealth around, too, especially in the bars and restaurants.

You Might Be a Native Outer Banker If …

This was an exciting week for Uncle Jack because he had to go to Philadelphia, which is something he hardly ever does. Now that he has been up there and back he remembers why it is something he hardly ever does.

He did get to do something he has wanted to do for a long time, which was to visit the Brandywine Museum in Chadd's Ford near Philadelphia, where they have many original paintings by some of Uncle Jack's favorite artists such as N.C. Wyeth and Andrew Wyeth and Jamie Wyeth who are various members of the famous Wyeth family who for some reason all turned out to be terrific artists when they grew up.

Uncle Jack is pretty sure that one reason for their success was that they painted pictures where you could tell what it was you were looking at when they got through, such as a dog or a barn. It is not easy to find pictures like that any more so they have a really good niche in the art market. If Uncle Jack could get one of the Wyeths to paint him some pictures of Hatteras lighthouse he would be on easy street in no time.

Anyway, that was the high point of his trip to Philadelphia except for the drive back down Route 13 on the Eastern Shore.

There was still a long way to go to Nags Head so Uncle Jack lapsed into thinking about some way he could get rich and famous without working and it occurred to him that maybe he could rip off Jeff Foxworthy, who does all those jokes about "rednecks" such as "You might be a redneck if you go to family reunions to meet girls" and many others of that ilk.

What he could do is write a book called *You Might Be a Native Outer Banker If* ..., which he could sell in all the better T-shirt and souvenir shops all up and down the Outer Banks and if they each sold one copy Uncle Jack would be rich and famous overnight.

For example, Mrs. Uncle Jack came up with:

- "You might be a native if you know that 'Hatteras' rhymes with 'mattress.'"
- "You might be a native if you have slept through a dozen hurricane evacuations."
- "You might be a native if you have never climbed Jockey's Ridge or swam in the ocean."
- "You might be a native if there is a recipe for

Beach cottages and small motels linger in the memory, while the spectre of modern "McMansions" looms.

boiled drum on your refrigerator door."
- "You might be a native if you have never bought a bloodworm."
- Or "You might be a native if at least six of your relatives work for the county."

Anyway, they ran out of ideas by the time they got to the bridge-tunnel by which time Uncle Jack had decided that this is definitely not the way to fame and fortune. Native 'Bankers are not rednecks and Uncle Jack is not Jeff Foxworthy so he is going to have to keep on working for a living for a while longer.

Uncle Jack's First Annual
State of the Outer Banks Address

Fellow Outer Bankers,

As we stand at the (choose one: threshold, brink, precipice) of another glorious Season in the Sun, let us pause for a moment to examine together the state of our beloved sandspit. Even the cynics and naysayers in our midst will agree that the past year was one of unprecedented growth, prosperity and progress and other good stuff like that. Consider the following economic indicators:

FOREIGN TRADE: Never has the Outer Banks enjoyed a more favorable balance of trade with the outside world than it does today. Latest Chamber of Commerce figures show that our mainland visitors spent far more on T-shirts, lighthouse replicas and ceramic seagulls last year than Outer Bankers spent at Sam's Club and Circuit City put together.

While it is unfortunate that the resulting surplus had to be divided amongst so many deserving merchants and that many therefore find themselves in straitened circumstances, they should take heart from the fact that only a few dozen new shops just like theirs will be opening this summer.

THE ENVIRONMENT: Last year saw tremendous progress toward the worthy goal of eliminating what is perhaps the Number One public health menace of the Outer Banks, namely flying sand. Uncle Jack is pleased to report that last year alone more than 27 square miles of unhealthy sand dunes, a major source of airborne particles, were brought under control through the copious application of asphalt and concrete. He is now able to predict with complete confidence that by the year 2030 the scourge of flying sand will be naught an unpleasant memory in the minds of a handful of surviving citizens.

Uncle Jack must admit that in spite of the best efforts of our enlightened lawmakers a few environmental challenges remain. The Atlantic Ocean, of course, is one of them. Year after year the ocean continues to demonstrate callous disregard for one of our most cherished and fundamental principles—the basic human right of property owners to build fourteen-bedroom rental houses wherever they please.

Uncle Jack is sure that you will agree that it is time to take whatever measures may be necessary to put the ocean in its place and therefore he is pleased to reveal at this time his "Master Plan to Stem the Tide At No Cost to the Taxpayers of Dare County."

Phase 1 of this simple but elegant strategy calls for the immediate replenishment of the South Nags Head beaches with sand from the unsightly pile known as Jockey's Ridge State Park (presently located at Milepost 12 directly across the Bypass from Austin's Fish Market.) This project will pay for itself through the sale of multiple millions of dollars' worth of oceanfront lots thus created.

Space does not permit further elucidation of Uncle Jack's Master Plan at this time but you may rest assured he will stay the course until it is accomplished come hell or high water. Especially high water.

OBX

Bed
and
Breakfasts

Uncle Jack read in the paper last week where they might pass a law so ordinary people could have tourists come and stay in their homes overnight and also they could feed them breakfast in the morning.

The reason is that some people are worried there won't be enough motel rooms to go around next summer when all the tourists come to Manteo to look at the big hole in the ground where the *Current* used to be.

The paper said a lot of motel and restaurant owners are not too thrilled about this "bed and breakfast" idea because they think that some of the houses the tourists would stay in might not be too clean. That is what they say they are worried about anyway and Uncle Jack would be the last one to wonder if that is the real reason.

If you want to know the truth, Uncle Jack

thinks this bed and breakfast idea is very good because he personally believes that a little dirt never hurt anybody.

That is something that he and Mrs. Uncle Jack really see eye-to-eye on, too. They are still using the same vacuum cleaner bag they got for a wedding present more than 29 years ago and it is not even half full yet.

The best thing about a bed and breakfast place, though is that it is cheap, and anything that is cheap is OK with Uncle Jack. "Cheap is best" is one of his favorite mottos along with "A little dirt never hurt anybody" and "I'll drink to that."

Bed and breakfast is something Uncle Jack knows a lot about, too, because before he settled down once and for all on the Outer Banks he used to be quite a world traveler and he has stayed in bed and breakfast places many times without any harmful effects that he knows of.

For one thing he learned how to share a bathroom with complete strangers and that is something that has really come in handy during the houseguest season.

Most of the bed and breakfast places he stayed in seemed to be about as clean as the average motel and the owners were at least as social as the average desk clerk and the breakfasts were often very interesting, to say the least.

If you want to know the truth, one of the best meals Uncle Jack ever ate was the breakfast he had at a "B&B" in Plymouth, England, where he went once because somebody told him that is where Columbus started out from when he discovered America.

Uncle Jack never did find a statue of Columbus in Plymouth, England, but he will never forget the breakfast he had there because it was the first time he had ever tasted fried bread.

You may not think that fried bread sounds like very much but Uncle Jack is here to tell you that if he could ever figure out how to fry bread like they do in Plymouth, England, he would be a rich man today instead of what he actually is. There would be an Uncle Jack's Fried Bread restaurant every two miles on the Bypass for one thing.

Uncle Jack really hopes they pass that bed and breakfast law because he is pretty sure a lot of tourists from faraway places like New Jersey and

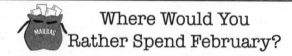

Where Would You Rather Spend February?

Dear Uncle Jack,

I have always heard that the middle of February is the absolute pits on the Outer Banks. How's it going down there anyway?

Chilly Billy
Akron, Ohio

Dear Chilly,

Uncle Jack can tell you think that things are really grim down here.

Greensboro could learn a lot by staying in ordinary people's houses instead of motels which when you get inside of them you could think you were still in New Jersey or Greensboro.

Also, having breakfast in an ordinary Outer Banks home could be just as exciting for a tourist from up north as eating fried bread in Plymouth, England, was for Uncle Jack.

Uncle Jack used to live up north and he knows there are thousands of people up there who have never tasted a Krispy Kreme donut much less washed a few down with a cold Pepsi.

That is the kind of breakfast that can make a person forget all about ham and eggs or French toast.

Not to mention fried bread.

He is writing this on Sunday, February 12, at 9 a.m. and the temperature is already 70 and there is no wind and the sun is shining and there is not a cloud in the sky.

The swans and geese look like they are getting ready to head north and the weatherman says we are in for another week like this before spring arrives so it doesn't look like Uncle Jack is going to get to use his new sled at all this winter.

Enjoy the snow while you can up there in Akron.

Happy shoveling,
Uncle Jack

High
on
the Hog

This was the week of the Nags Head Surf Fishing Club's annual Pig Pickin' and Social Hour so Uncle Jack does not have to tell you what kind of a week it was for him. As far as he is concerned this week ranks right up there with Thanksgiving in the eating department every year.

There is no way he can tell you how good the pig was this year except to say it was just as good as last year. If you were at the pig pickin' last year you will know what Uncle Jack is talking about but if you were not there you are out of luck. Words fail him sometimes and this is one of them.

While he was eating his second plate he was thinking that this might be where they got that old saying about eating "high on the hog." Actually it is hard to tell if you are eating high on the hog or not because they chop it up pretty good. But no matter where it came from, high or low, it was all good and that applies to the fixin's too.

As far as Uncle Jack is concerned the Spring Pig Pickin' is one of the premier events on the Outer Banks social calendar and he could tell that a lot of other people feel the same way because everybody there was wearing shoes.

Uncle Jack tried out his brand new state-of-the-art Pro Keds which have the Velcro tabs instead of laces. He is pleased to tell you they held up real well and gave him very good traction even late in the evening when the floor started getting fairly greasy in spots.

Just about everybody who is anybody was there including numerous important political leaders who were easy to spot because they were trying to talk and shake hands and eat pig all at the same time so they tended to look a little more awkward than they really are.

Anyway it made Uncle Jack feel good to think that a person like himself who never even saw a bluefish until he was almost 40 years old could be a member in good standing of a high-ranking organization like the Nags Head Surf Fishing Club. Only in America, and that is for sure.

OBX

Changeover Day

Uncle Jack is pleased to report that today (Sunday, June 14) is one of those Outer Banks days that is so perfect in every respect that he cannot think of a single thing worth grumbling about. It is so perfect that if he were a nice person he would wish that everybody in the world could be here today to enjoy what he is enjoying.

Then he remembers what it was like on the Bypass yesterday and he realizes that most of the people in the world, at least those who own cars, probably are already here.

The sky is cloudless, the ocean calm and brilliant blue. A light breeze from the north is just cool enough to fool sun worshippers into thinking they are getting great tans instead of third-degree burns.

Uncle Jack is sitting in his favorite rocking chair on his upper deck whence he enjoys watching the endless fascinating parade of God's creatures—the pelicans, the gulls, the porpoises, and especially the tourists who rent all the houses in his neighborhood.

From now until late fall the ebb and flow of tourists will be as regular and predictable as the ocean tide. Uncle Jack lives in a Sunday-to-Sunday neighborhood, so he gets to observe the whole fascinating changeover cycle every week on his day off.

Each Sunday morning the cars that have dozed in all the nearby driveways for the past week suddenly become energized again for the trip home. Their tanned owners struggle grimly to force back into them the same mass of stuff they unloaded so happily only seven days earlier, which seems to have mysteriously doubled in size.

This is not a happy task and Uncle Jack has observed that it often leads to spousal discord of considerable magnitude. He thinks perhaps the expression "hell on wheels" was coined to describe some tourists' return trips to Pittsburgh or Buffalo or wherever.

Eventually the packing is completed and the

husband takes his place behind the wheel, where he waits for his wife to finish cleaning the house so she won't be ashamed when the professional cleaners come here to get the house ready for the next renters. He waits and waits and waits. The car is not out of the driveway and already the kids are screaming to go the bathroom. With nothing better to do, Dad screams back.

Eventually Mom appears, car doors slam, Dad burns rubber on the way out of the driveway and peace descends upon the neighborhood again. At some point the cleaners arrive, make a brief inspection of the departing housewife's efforts, load the left-behind perishables into their industrial-sized coolers, wheel the overflowing garbage can out to the street and depart as quickly as they came. Rarely do they seem to break a sweat.

Hours later a car creeps slowly up Uncle Jack's street while the occupants try, like lottery players, to match numbers on houses with numbers on their rental packets. The weekly cycle begins again.

Remembering

 ## The Good
Old Days

Dear Uncle Jack,

You mentioned once that you first came to the
Outer Banks in 1969 or thereabouts. Did you wash up
in a shipwreck or what? What was it like around here in
the old days?

Jenny Ecks
Colington Harbour

Dear Jenny,

Your questions have thrown Uncle Jack into
a veritable fit of nostalgia. He did indeed discover the
Outer Banks in 1969 and for him it gave new meaning
to the old saw that life begins at 40.

He did not wash up on the beach but that might
have been preferable to running the gauntlet of hog
farms that used to line the highway in Currituck County
before Progress hit and turned it into a five-mile-long
strip shopping center and billboard arcade.

*"Sorry, Honey. I'll be about forty years late
for dinner tonight."*

Uncle Jack will never forget the first time he crossed the old two-lane Wright Memorial Bridge and saw Roanoke Sound and Jockey's Ridge for the first time. The view is still breathtaking and so is the traffic.

Turning south on the "Bypass" in 1969 he drove for miles before he saw a building. He can't remember what building it was and he would never be able to find it anyway now that the Bypass no longer bypasses anything.

His destination was the First Colony Inn on the oceanfront near the 13 milepost. Today he would have to look between the highways at the 16 milepost and how it got there is an amazing story.

He bought groceries at Harris's Grocery, now a rib joint, just down the street from the post office, now the unemployment office, and he bought fish from Midgett's Seafood, now defunct, just down the street from Austin's gas station, now Austin's Seafood. "*Plus ca change, plus la meme chose*" as they say in gay Paris—and straight Paris, too, for that matter.

He bought beer at Bell's store, now a Mexican restaurant, just down the street from the Foosball Palace, now eight upscale rental houses, and a short walk from the magnificent Old Nagsheader Hotel, now eight more upscale rental houses.

For essential supplies like duct tape and fly screen he drove to Virginia Dare Hardware in Kitty Hawk, now an upscale eatery with cool jazz on Wednesday nights but not a can of WD-40 in the place.

He walked his dogs in the vast, empty Epstein Tract, now the Village at Nags Head complete with 18-hole golf course and upwards of 500 upscale rental houses cluttering the dunes.

He is happy to report that some things haven't changed a bit. He still buys his spiritual beverages at the same old ABC store on the Bypass and the fish sandwiches at Sam and Omie's still taste as good as they did in 1969, and most of those grand old cottages on the Beach Road in Nags Head are still there, even though most of them have been moved back from the ocean since then.

Ah yes, the ocean. It's still there, too, and it hasn't changed at all. He can still sit and stare at the ocean for hours and it's 1969 all over again.

Uncle Jack

PLANNING TO BUY A PIECE OF THE OUTER BANKS?

BEFORE YOU MAKE THAT DOWN PAYMENT
YOU OWE IT TO YOURSELF TO VISIT

SHIFTING SANDS

THE EXCITING NEW CONDOMINIUM NORTH
OF DUCK. WE OFFER THE LOWEST PRICED LOTS AT
THE BEST TERMS IN THE LAST REMAINING UNSPOILED
SECTION OF THE OUTER BANKS··· SEEING IS BELIEVING
DRIVE NORTH ON ROUTE 31 TO THE END OF THE
PAVED ROAD···CONTINUE NORTH FOLLOWING THE
CLEARLY MARKED RUTS UNTIL YOU GET STUCK.
WAIT FOR OUR TOW TRUCK WHICH WILL PULL YOU
THE REST OF THE WAY TO··· SHIFTING SANDS.

SHIFTING SANDS
" YOU'LL GET STUCK ON US"

ILLUSTRATION
CREDITS

(All illustrations are sketch artwork unless otherwise indicated.)

ILLUSTRATION CREDITS

(Continued)

ACKNOWLEDGMENTS

THIS COLLECTION of Jack Sandberg's writings required Jack, of course. I thank him for his fine writing, for conveying the rights to me, and for assisting in preparing this volume. The defunct *Outer Banks Current* and *Outer Banks Sentinel* should be thanked for putting him in print in the first place. And so should *Boomer* magazine, for allowing us to reprint a later piece. I also need to acknowledge an unsung hero: Gene Varble of Kill Devil Hills, a fan who simply showed up on Jack's doorstep one day and presented him with a scrapbook of his early columns; the scrapbook helped supplement Jack's files. Susan and Jack Sandberg, and Vicki McAllister, proofreaders extraordinaire, corrected my bad typing.

Three talented artists deserve credit. Tom Butler and Mike Lucas crafted the sketch drawings for Jack's booklets in the 1980s and '90s. Most are included here. (The afore-mentioned Vicki colorized a Lucas sketch for the cover.) Then Stuart Parks II created a new batch for this volume that also perfectly capture the spirit of Jack's works. In addition, several existing sketches were found that complemented it, and rights were secured from their artists.

Finally, of course, come you readers, whether you are new to these works or have been a fan for decades. It is for you that Uncle Jack wrote.

RAY McALLISTER

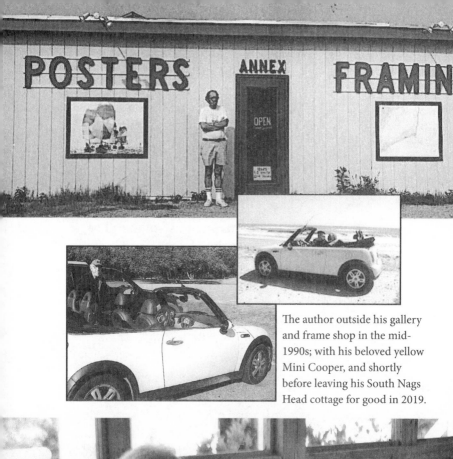

The author outside his gallery and frame shop in the mid-1990s; with his beloved yellow Mini Cooper, and shortly before leaving his South Nags Head cottage for good in 2019.

ABOUT THE AUTHOR

J ACK SANDBERG, a native of Wisconsin, lived
on the Outer Banks of North Carolina for much of
four decades before moving to Baltimore in 2019. Earlier,
he had been an elementary school teacher and principal,
served on a U.S. Navy destroyer during the Korean War, and
taught at Carnegie Mellon University in Pittsburgh for seventeen years before finding the courage to chuck it all and
move to Nags Head.

In 1980, he became a reporter for the
Outer Banks Current, a weekly newspaper in
Nags Head. He later served as the paper's
editor for five months while the publishers tried to find a competent journalist.

He contributed more than 400 "Uncle Jack" columns
to the *Current* before running out of ideas in 1988. Beginning in 1996, "Uncle Jack" next appeared regularly in the
Outer Banks Sentinel. Some columns also were collected
for three booklets, each entitled, with diminishing creativity, *Uncle Jack's Outer Banks*. His humor also appeared in
Pittsburgher Magazine, Pennsylvania Illustrated, Decor, and other equally famous publications. Later, *Boomer* magazine
found him funny enough to publish not once but twice.

With his wife, Dr. Sue Maloney, he operated Yellowhouse
Gallery, a fixture on the Beach Road in Nags Head since
1970. They lived in South Nags Head where they enjoyed
a constantly improving ocean view as neighboring houses
toppled into the sea. Ardent lovers of traditional jazz, they
often hung out in New Orleans during the off-season.

The author's proudest moment was his graduation from Ashland (Wisconsin) High School in
1948 (right). The rest, he says, was gravy.

Books That Endure

BEACH GLASS
Books

BeachGlassBooks.com